AMONG THE CANADIAN ALPS

LECTOR HOUSE PUBLIC DOMAIN WORKS

AMONG THE CANADIAN ALPS

LAWRENCE JOHNSTONE BURPEE

ISBN: 978-93-5420-001-4

Published: 1914

LECTOR HOUSE LLP
E-MAIL: lectorpublishing@gmail.com

BERG LAKE AND TUMBLING GLACIER

R. C. W. Lett

AMONG THE CANADIAN ALPS

BY

LAWRENCE J. BURPEE
F.R.G.S.

WITH FOUR ILLUSTRATIONS IN COLOUR
FORTY-FIVE REPRODUCTIONS FROM
PHOTOGRAPHS AND FIVE MAPS

MCMXIV

PREFACE

The writer takes this opportunity of gratefully acknowledging his indebtedness to Mr. J. B. Harkin, Commissioner of Dominion Parks, Col. Maynard Rogers, Superintendent of Jasper Park, and Mr. Arthur O. Wheeler, Director of the Alpine Club of Canada, for valued assistance in gathering material for this book; to Mr. Walter D. Wilcox, Sir James Outram, Dr. A. P. Coleman, Dr. J. W. A. Hickson, Rev. George Kinney, Dr. Charles E. Fay and Mr. P. D. McTavish, for permission to quote from their books and articles on the Rocky Mountains; and to Miss Mary M. Vaux, Mrs. Mary T. S. Schäffer, Mr. W. H. P. Lett, Mr. Arthur O. Wheeler, Mr. H. W. Craver, Rev. George Kinney, Mr. P. D. McTavish, Mr. James F. Porter, Mr. P. L. Tait, Mr. John Woodruff, Mr. A. Knechtel, Messrs. G. and W. Fear, the Canadian Pacific Railway Company and the Grand Trunk Pacific Railway Company, for permission to reproduce photographs of Rocky Mountain scenery and climbing and other incidents.

OTTAWA, CANADA
October, 1914

CONTENTS

LIST OF ILLUSTRATIONS

Page

LIST OF MAPS

I

THE LURE OF THE MOUNTAINS

WHAT is the peculiar charm of that mighty, snow-capped sea of mountains, whose stupendous waves tossed far into the heavens seem ever about to overwhelm the level wheat-fields of Western Canada? The lure of the mountains defies analysis, but it is surely there with its irresistible appeal to all in whom the spirit of romance is not quite dead. It stirs the blood strangely when, far out on the plains of Alberta, you get your first glimpse of the Canadian Alps—a line of white, glittering peaks just above the horizon, infinitely remote and ethereal, something altogether apart from the prosaic world about you of grain and cattle, neat farmhouse and unsightly elevator.

As you follow the course of the sun, the peaks loom gradually up into the sky and dominate the scene, but still retain the atmosphere of another world. The rolling foothills in the foreground, like spent waves from the storm-tossed sea, seem tangible and comprehensible, but beyond and above the dark ramparts of the outer range, the towering outer wave of the mountains, float silvery outlines that seem to be the fabric of some other and purer world. Doubt may come with the marvellously clear and hardening light of the western day, but at sunrise, and peculiarly at sunset, the last shreds of uncertainty are swept away. Not of this earth is that dream of fairyland poised mysteriously in the upper air, glowing in exquisite tints, soft as a summer cloud; a realm of the spirit to which one might hope to journey over the path of a rainbow.

One who has seen this vision may not resist the insistent call to explore the mountain world, to discover what lies beyond the frowning battlements that guard this other realm. The call has been working in the hearts of men for generations. They came alone in the early days, each man fighting his way up through some doorway that led into the heart of the Glittering Mountains. Only the stout of heart might then win through, for this Wonderland was guarded close on every side. Pitfalls awaited the unwary. The explorer must cut his own trail through the wilderness, cross icy torrents, climb alpine passes, find a way through networks of fallen timber, face perils and discomforts every hour of the day. And yet there was something alluring, something that drew him on, and brought him back again to these high fastnesses; something that he could not understand, but that was none the less imperative. That same spell is as potent to-day, but most of the barriers are down, and where once men came singly or in twos and threes, paying heavily in labour and peril for the joys they found in the mountains, thousands now follow at just enough cost to themselves to give spice to the experience.

Mary M. Vaux, W. S. Vaux and G. Vaux, Jr.

MOUNT TEMPLE

The history of the Canadian Alps, so far as White Men have had anything to do with it, dates back to the closing years of the French Régime in Canada. It is characteristic of the race that gave to the world such heroic figures as those of Champlain and La Salle and La Vérendrye, that while the infamous Bigot and the egotistical and brainless Vaudreuil were gambling away an empire in the New World, tireless and unselfish explorers were carrying the boundaries of that empire far out toward the setting sun.

It was in the year 1751 that the Chevalier de Niverville, with a small party of French *voyageurs*, pushed his way up the muddy waters of the Saskatchewan, and built Fort Lajonquière in the foothills of the Rocky Mountains. Niverville was not the discoverer of the mighty range that runs like a backbone throughout the length of North America. He had been anticipated some years before by a fellow-countryman, La Vérendrye, son of the patriotic explorer who had devoted his life to western discovery for the glory of his native land. Niverville, however, was the first White Man to look upon that portion of the mountains now known as the Canadian Rockies.

One wonders what his impressions were as he gazed out to the westward over that bewildering scene. As a Canadian officer he had served in the expeditions against the New England Colonies, and was therefore familiar with the mountains of New Hampshire and Vermont, as well as with his own Laurentian Hills, but what preparation were these for such awe-inspiring majesty? Range piled upon range to the westward, soaring up and up in vast towers and domes and spires, and extending north and south to the utmost limits of vision, they must have seemed to Niverville an impregnable fortification designed to bar all further progress in this direction.

Niverville was not the man, however, to be daunted by even the most formidable natural obstacle, and he was not without evidence that a way might be found through the mountains to the shores of that Western Sea for which he and many other Canadian explorers had been searching, even since the days of Champlain. While at Fort Lajonquière a party of Indians visited him, from whom he learned that they had traded with a strange tribe whose home was far to the westward, beyond the great barrier, and who spoke of White Men that they had seen on the sea coast. Niverville no doubt made plans for an expedition through the mountains, but they came to nothing. His leader, Saint-Pierre, was having trouble with the Indians at his fort on the Assiniboine; Niverville was recalled, and before long the entire party of French explorers were making their way back to far-off Quebec, to help Montcalm in his last desperate effort to save New France.

In 1754, and again in 1772, officers of the Hudson's Bay Company made journeys of exploration from York Factory, on the western shores of Hudson Bay, to the country of the Blackfoot Indians, among the foothills of the Rocky Mountains; but it was not until 1793 that any White Man was daring enough to penetrate their fastnesses. In that year Alexander Mackenzie, who had four years earlier descended the river that bears his name, to the shores of the Arctic Ocean, forced his way through the Peace River Pass, and after suffering great hardships, stood at last beside the waters of the Pacific, fulfilling at last the dream of French explorers of an overland route to the Western Sea.

Within the next few years discoveries followed thick and fast. The North West Company, the Canadian rival of the Hudson's Bay Company in the western fur trade, was reaching out eagerly for new fields to conquer, and the more adventurous of its officers, scouting far ahead of the main army, became more explorers than fur-traders. Mackenzie was himself a partner of the North West Company, and where he led others soon followed, breaking new trails through the mountains, leaving the level plains and comparatively sparse vegetation of the eastern side, and coming down into the almost tropical luxuriance of the Pacific slope.

David Thompson, the astronomer of the North West Company, was the first to find a way through the mountains in the neighbourhood of the Kicking Horse Pass route, or the main line of the Canadian Pacific Railway. In 1800 he made his way over to the Columbia Valley, perhaps by what was later known as the Simpson Pass; and the same year Duncan McGillivray found a route farther north by Howse Pass, named after Jasper Howse, another Rocky Mountain explorer. Simon Fraser, who had followed Mackenzie through the Peace Pass, in 1808 explored the river that bears his name from the mountains to the sea, descending its terrific canyons in a frail canoe.

At the very time that Fraser was making his way down this river, Thompson was exploring the Kootenay and the Columbia. Two years afterward the latter discovered the Athabaska Pass, which for many years was to remain the principal highway of the fur-traders back and forth through the mountains. Often enough the mountains above the pass must have looked down upon the picturesque cavalcade of traders, carrying goods over to the posts in New Caledonia or down the Columbia, or bringing back the "returns" as the cargoes of furs were called. One can picture the long string of pack-horses climbing up the pass, with the cheerful philosophy (or diabolical cunning) of the Indian cayuse, urged forward by fluent traders. One can see, too, at nightfall, the camp-fires in the mountains; horses, browsing contentedly; men lounging about waiting for their supper, perhaps fresh venison, or the old stand-by pemmican; and later, pipe and story and song—the beautiful old *chansons* of French Canada with their haunting refrains:

> A la claire fontaine
> M'en allant promener,
> J'ai trouvé l'eau si belle
> Que je m'y suis baigné.
> *I' ya longtemps que je t'aime,*
> *Jamais je ne t'oublierai.*

or—

> Derrier' chez nous, ya-t-un étang,
> *En roulant ma boule.*
> Trois beaux canards s'en vont baignant,
> *En roulant ma boule.*
> *Rouli, roulant, ma boule roulant,*
> *En roulant ma boule roulant,*

En roulant ma boule.

John Woodruff

VERMILION LAKE AND MOUNT RUNDLE

After this initial age of exploration, most of the credit of which belongs to the men of the North West Company, we come to a period of travel. Some of the rarest and at the same time most interesting books of travel in Northwestern America are those which describe overland journeys to and from the Pacific by way of one or other of the famous gateways through the Canadian Rockies. Such a book is Gabriel Franchère's narrative including an account of his trip through the mountains in 1814; another is that of Ross Cox, who with Franchère was concerned in the dramatic events connected with the history of Astoria, of which Washington Irving wrote such an entertaining and thoroughly unreliable account. Ross Cox crossed the mountains three years after Franchère.

Another little-known narrative is that of Sir George Simpson's expedition of 1825. Sir George Simpson was then Governor of the Hudson's Bay Company, and like Jehu he drove furiously. He travelled in what was known as a light canoe, manned with picked boatmen famous for speed, skill and endurance; they were off at daylight or earlier, and did not camp before nightfall. In his journeys across the continent, by the great water routes of the fur-trade, the Governor's canoe bore about the same relation to the regular brigades that the Twentieth Century Limited does to a freight train.

One of the most fascinating of the narratives of this period is Paul Kane's *Wanderings of an Artist among the Indians of North America*. Kane was a Toronto artist, who travelled across the continent studying the manners and customs of the various tribes, and making a series of most delightful sketches of them and of their country. His comments on the natives and their habits are shrewd and entertaining, and if written to-day would sometimes be thought much too frank for publication. Kane crossed the Athabaska Pass in 1846, and returned the same way the following year.

Five or six years earlier Sir George Simpson again traversed the mountains, by the pass that bears his name, in the course of his famous journey around the world. The journeys of Father De Smet, the western missionary, of the Earl of Southesk, of Milton and Cheadle, and of William Francis Butler, to mention only a few of the more prominent, belong to the same general period.

Butler went through the Peace River Pass, and at its eastern entrance climbed a steep hill known as the Buffalo's Head to get his first wide view of the mountains. He tried to describe what he saw, but admitted the futility of the attempt.

"Not more wooden," he says, "are the ark animals of our childhood, than the words in which man would clothe the images of that higher nature which the Almighty has graven into the shapes of lonely mountains! Put down your wooden woods bit by bit; throw in colour here, a little shade there, touch it up with sky and cloud, cast about it that perfume of blossom or breeze, and in Heaven's name what does it come to after all? Can the eye wander away, away, away until it is lost in blue distance as a lark is lost in blue heaven, but the sight still drinks the beauty of the landscape, though the source of the beauty be unseen, as the source of the music which falls from the azure depths of the sky.

"That river coming out broad and glittering from the dark mountains, and vanishing into yon profound chasm with a roar which reaches up even here—

billowy seas of peaks and mountains beyond number away there to south and west—that huge half dome which lifts itself above all others sharp and clear cut against the older dome of heaven! Turn east, look out into that plain—that endless plain where the pine-trees are dwarfed to speargrass and the prairie to a meadow-patch—what do you see? Nothing, poor blind reader, nothing, for the blind is leading the blind; and all this boundless range of river and plain, ridge and prairie, rocky precipice and snow-capped sierra, is as much above my poor power of words, as He who built this mighty nature is higher still than all."

Yet so insistent is the charm of the mountains, as he makes his way ever deeper into their secret recesses, that he must try once more to put his impressions into words:

"Wonderful things to look at are these white peaks, perched up so high above our world. They belong to us, yet they are not of us. The eagle links them to the earth; the cloud carries to them the message of the sky; the ocean sends them her tempest; the air rolls her thunders beneath their brows, and launches her lightnings from their sides; the sun sends them his first greeting, and leaves them his latest kiss. Yet motionless they keep their crowns of snow, their glacier crests of jewels, and dwell among the stars heedless of time or tempest."

Up to the year of 1858 travel in the Rocky Mountains was confined to one or other of the passes. Men did not wander off the beaten trails, but hurried through east or west. Between 1858 and 1860 the members of the Palliser Expedition, and particularly that tireless explorer, Dr. James Hector, pushed into the very heart of the mountains, discovering new passes, tracing rivers to their sources, and for the first time giving the world some idea of the wonderful region of peaks, lakes and valleys that lay beyond the western prairies. Among many other familiar place-names in the Canadian Rockies, that of Kicking Horse Pass was given by Dr. Hector, who on his first journey through the pass was nearly killed by a vicious horse. It has before now been suggested that a more appropriate name for this important route through the mountains would be that of the explorer himself.

The task so splendidly initiated by Captain Palliser and his associates of exploring and mapping the Canadian Rockies was afterward taken up by the officers of the Canadian Geological Survey and the Topographical Survey of Canada, and is still in progress.

Canadian Pacific Railway Company

THE THREE SISTERS, ROCKY MOUNTAINS PARK

Canadian Pacific Railway Company

MOUNT WAPTA AND SUMMIT LAKE

(Yoho Park)

One may round out this very brief survey of the opening up of the Canadian Alps, the Wonderlands of the Canadian West, by mentioning some recent expeditions of a group of explorers whose object was rather recreation than science; who saw in these mountains a boundless playground where tired men and women of the cities might find rest and pleasure, where unclimbed peaks rise on every side to tempt the more energetic and repay them with marvellous impressions of unforgettable splendour, where snowbound passes lead one over into green valleys holding in their embrace lakes of the most exquisite colouring, where the mountain goat and the bighorn gaze down upon you from dizzy heights or scamper up the face of impossible precipices, and the silvertip lumbers off the trail with ponderous dignity, where the day's tramp brings endless variety of towering cliff and snowy summit, cathedral aisles in the primæval forest, falling curtains of mist from gigantic glaciers, chaotic slopes of rock and alpine meadows dressed in all the colours of the rainbow, where the camp-fire brings perfect content and a spirit of comradeship unknown in the cities, where the mountain air puts new life into you, fills you with wholesome optimism, makes you realise as you never did before that the world is good, good to look upon and good to live upon.

One need only mention the titles of some of the books in which these expeditions are described to suggest the spirit that animates them: Hornaday's *Camp-fires in the Canadian Rockies*, Schaffers's *Old Indian Trails*, Outram's *In the Heart of the Canadian Rockies*, Green's *Among the Selkirk Glaciers*. If we add the wonderfully-illustrated work of Walter D. Wilcox, and the narratives of Stutfield and Collie, Coleman, Baillie-Grohman, and a few others, we have a little library of Canadian Alpine literature that will be a revelation to any one who has not yet become familiar with the irresistible appeal of this land of pure delight.

A word remains to be said, and it may as well be said here as elsewhere, as to routes—how to get to the Canadian National Parks. From Eastern Canada, and the Atlantic seaboard, probably the most convenient route is the direct transcontinental line of the Canadian Pacific Railway from Montreal, and by that route unquestionably the most comfortable train is the well-known "Imperial Limited." From Toronto, or points south of Toronto in the United States, the "Pacific Express" of the Canadian Pacific Railway offers a direct route to the Mountains. If your starting-point is in the Middle West, it will be well to take the route from Chicago to Winnipeg and join the "Imperial Limited" there; or the more direct line from Chicago to the main line of the Canadian Pacific Railway at Moosejaw. All these routes will bring you to the eastern portal of the mountains at Calgary, and on to Banff and other points in the Parks. If you are bound for Jasper Park in the north, any of the three transcontinental railways, the Grand Trunk Pacific, Canadian Pacific, or Canadian Northern, will take you direct from Winnipeg to Edmonton, and you can get in to the Park by either the Grand Trunk Pacific or Canadian Northern.

If your starting-point is on the Pacific Coast the Canadian Pacific Railway from Vancouver is the direct route, or you may join the main line from the south at several points east of Vancouver. By the autumn of 1914 the Grand Trunk Pacific will be completed to its Pacific terminus, Prince Rupert, and the Canadian Northern may also be ready for traffic to Vancouver before the end of the year. Round trips will then be possible taking in all the Canadian Mountain Parks: From Calgary by Canadian Pacific Railway to Rocky Mountain Park, Yoho Park and Glacier Park, and on to Vancouver. From Vancouver north by boat to Prince Rupert, and by Grand Trunk Pacific east to Robson Park and Jasper Park; or possibly direct from Vancouver by Canadian Northern to the same parks. From Jasper Park the return to Calgary would be by Edmonton and the Canadian Pacific Railway branch line.

II

THE NATIONAL PARKS OF CANADA

THE last spike in the first of Canada's transcontinental roads, the Canadian Pacific Railway, was driven at Craigillachie, British Columbia, in 1885. Two years later, after a memorable debate in the House of Commons, an Act of Parliament was passed setting apart for the use and enjoyment of the people of the young Dominion a national park in the heart of the Rocky Mountains. Thus was initiated a policy which has since been developed upon broad and generous lines, and which will ultimately give Canada an unrivalled system of magnificent natural playgrounds.

The first park, as created in 1887, covered an area of 260 square miles, with the little station of Banff, on the Canadian Pacific Railway, as headquarters. In 1902 the area was enlarged to 5,000 square miles, but reduced again in 1911, under the terms of the Forest Reserves and Parks Act, to 1,800 square miles. The object of the reduction was apparently to confine the park to an area that could be efficiently administered with the existing staff. It is understood, however, that in view of the extraordinary popularity of this wonderful mountain region, steps will be taken before long to re-establish the boundaries of 1902. The wisdom of such a move cannot be doubted. The increased cost of maintenance would be comparatively slight, and the advantages would be enormous. It would make accessible the exceedingly interesting country north of the present park boundaries with its great alpine peaks, snow-fields and glaciers, its beautiful valleys, lakes, mountain streams and waterfalls; it would help to preserve from destruction by vandalism or sheer carelessness many of the scenic beauties of the region; and would give to the wild animals of the mountains a further lease of life.

Mary M. Vaux, W. S. Vaux, and G. Vaux, Jr.

MOUNT LEFROY AND LAKE LOUISE

(After a midsummer snowstorm)

Since the establishment of the first reservation, known officially as Rocky Mountains Park, and popularly as the Banff Park, several other similar districts have been set apart. Immediately west of Rocky Mountains Park, but on the British Columbia side of the main range, is Yoho Park, with an area of about 560 square miles. The boundaries of this park also will, it is hoped, be enlarged in the near future. West again, and still following the main line of the Canadian Pacific Railway, we come to Glacier Park, in the Selkirk Mountains, with an area of 468 square miles. Farther north, on the main line of the Grand Trunk Pacific Railway, the Canadian Government has lately established Jasper Park, with an area of 1,000 square miles. This, too, may be expanded to several times its present dimensions within the next few years.[1] It is possible also that a new park may be created between Rocky Mountain Park and Jasper Park, to embrace the little-known Brazeau River country and possibly the upper waters of the North Saskatchewan, with the great peaks that lie up toward the continental divide. Down near the International Boundary, at the extreme southwestern corner of the province of Alberta, is Waterton Lake Park. The present area is only sixteen square miles, but the Government is being strongly urged to extend its boundaries so as to make the reserve conterminous with Glacier Park on the United States side, thereby creating what would in effect be an international park.[2] North again, but still in the province of Alberta, are Buffalo Park and Elk Island Park, the former of 160 square miles, a little south of Wainwright, on the Grand Trunk Pacific Railway, and the latter, about the same area as Waterton Lake Park, near Lamont, on the Canadian Northern Railway. The former is the home of the famous herd of buffalo, now numbering over 1,200, most of which were purchased by the Dominion Government in 1907 from Michel Don Pablo of Missoula, Montana. The latter is a reservation for elk, moose and other large animals.

In addition to the proposed Brazeau Park, access to which would be provided by the Canadian Northern Railway, plans are being formulated for a new park west of Glacier, to include Mount Revelstoke and the surrounding region, and another on the Pacific Coast not far from the city of Vancouver, to include the country between the north arm of Burrard Inlet and Pitt River.

The somewhat peculiar boundaries of the Canadian National Parks may call for a word of explanation. It will be noticed that on their western, or rather southwestern, sides Rocky Mountains and Jasper Parks stop at the continental divide, or in other words at the boundary between Alberta and British Columbia. The explanation is this: when British Columbia came into the Dominion she retained control of the public lands within her borders; on the other hand when the province of Alberta was created her land remained vested in the Dominion. Consequently the federal authorities may establish national parks wherever they will on the Alberta side of the mountains, but have no jurisdiction on the British Columbia side except in one particular region. This is a strip of land forty miles wide, or twenty miles on each side of the Canadian Pacific Railway main line, extending from the summit of the Rocky Mountains to the Pacific Ocean. When British Columbia entered Confederation in 1871, one of the terms of union was that the new province should

[1] Increased in 1914 to 4,400 square miles.
[2] This has since been done, the present area of the park being 423 square miles.

be given railway connection with Eastern Canada. In fulfilment of this agreement, the Dominion granted the Canadian Pacific Railway a subsidy of $25,000,000 and 25,000,000 acres of land. British Columbia was also to give a money subsidy to the company, but finding it impossible to meet its obligations the Dominion assumed the burden in consideration of a grant of this forty-mile strip across the province. It is in this strip, therefore, that the Yoho and Glacier Parks have been located, as well as the proposed park at Burrard Inlet.

The policy of the Dominion Government in administering its national parks is to throw them wide open to the people, to provide convenient means of access to every point of interest within their boundaries, to preserve intact their natural beauties and safeguard their wild life, and to grant all visitors the widest liberty consistent with these objects and with the interests of the people themselves; in fact to provide the maximum of convenience and protection with the minimum of interference. Thanks largely to the intelligence, broad-mindedness and genuine enthusiasm of the officials in charge of the Parks, from the Commissioner in Ottawa to the Forest Ranger on duty in some remote corner of the reservation, the administration has been conspicuously successful, as every one will admit who has had the good fortune to visit any of these magnificent national playgrounds.

The extent to which the Parks administration is prepared to go in insuring the comfort and convenience of those who seek rest or pleasure in the mountains is admirably illustrated in the following extract from the Commissioner's Report:

"The Parks Branch policy necessarily relates to the quality of the service of whatever kind rendered by those dealing with the tourist: character of accommodation, avoidance of congestion, protection against extortion, provision of minor attractions to fill in between the nature trips, construction and maintenance of good roads and trails, special care in the matter of the dust nuisance and rough roads, supervision over sanitary conditions, water supply, horses and vehicles, guides, drivers, charges and rates, furnishing of full and reliable information, and, generally, the reduction of discomforts to a minimum and the administration of affairs so that the tourist shall be as satisfied with the treatment received while in the parks as he inevitably must be with the scenic wonders he has viewed."

The accommodation of the hotels in the parks is excellent in every way. In spite of their out-of-the-way situation they provide all the comforts and luxuries of city hotels, and at very moderate rates. There are several good hotels at Banff in the Rocky Mountains Park, the best of which is the Banff Springs Hotel, maintained by the Canadian Pacific Railway. The railway company also owns the very comfortable Chalet at Lake Louise, in the same park, as well as the hotels at Field, in Yoho Park, and Glacier, in Glacier Park. The Grand Trunk Pacific Railway has also decided to build hotels at Jasper and Miette Hot Springs, in Jasper Park, as well as at Grand Fork in Robson Park, within full view of the monarch of the Canadian Rockies, Mount Robson. Robson Park has recently been set apart by the Government of British Columbia. Its boundaries extended to the height of land where they run with those of Jasper Park.

One of the admirable features of the administration of the Canadian National

Parks is the leasing of lots on nominal terms, so that those who prefer home to hotel life may build their own cottages. At Banff you can obtain a lot for from $8.00 to $15.00 a year, according to position and area. The leases run for forty-two years, with the privilege of renewal for an equal period. The same privilege may be obtained in Jasper Park.

Canadian Pacific Railway Company

CATHEDRAL PEAK

(*From Kicking Horse Pass*)

R. C. W. Lett

MOOSE PASS

(On the Borders of Robson Park)

One of the principal activities of the Park administration is of course the building of roads and trails to the various points of interest, mountains, lakes, waterfalls, and so forth. The Canadian parks are still in their infancy from an administrative point of view, and an immense amount of work remains to be done before their innumerable points of beauty and grandeur are made conveniently accessible. Still it is possible to-day to reach all the principal peaks and valleys with a moderate expenditure of time and energy. In the four principal parks, Rocky Mountains, Yoho, Glacier and Jasper, there are now, 163 miles of good carriage road, and nearly 300 miles of trail, and this mileage will be largely increased within the next few years. It is the intention also to provide foot-paths to all the nearer points, with rest-houses, for those who prefer to wander about afoot.

An ambitious project closely associated with the parks is the automobile road from Calgary to Vancouver. This is being built through the co-operation of the Dominion Government, the provincial governments of Alberta and British Columbia, and the Canadian Pacific Railway. Portions of the road are already completed, and the balance has been surveyed and the necessary appropriations provided. The present coach road from Calgary to Banff will be improved to form the first link; and the Banff to Laggan road will be utilised as far as Castle Mountain. Here the automobile road turns up Little Vermilion Creek to Vermilion Pass, the boundary of Rocky Mountains Park on this side. From Vermilion Pass the road will cross the Briscoe Range by Sinclair Pass to Sinclair Hot Springs, and ascend the valley of the Columbia to Windermere Lake and the source of the Columbia. Crossing the spit of land that separates the Columbia from its mighty tributary the Kootenay, the road will follow the latter stream to Wardner, then turn west to Kootenay Lake and Nelson, cross the Columbia again after its huge bend to the north, and swing down to the international boundary at Grand Forks, where connection will no doubt be made some time with automobile roads from the south. From Grand Forks the road will follow a general westerly direction, crossing Okanagan River near Fairview, ascending the Similkameen, traversing the Hope Range and coming down the Coquihalla to Hope on the Fraser River, and descending the Fraser to Vancouver.

An alternative route runs west from Windermere, over the Wells Pass, crosses the Lardo country to Killarney at the head of the Lower Arrow Lake, thence up Fire Valley to the present wagon road near Monashee Mines, follows the road to Vernon and Grand Prairie, and by way of Douglas Lake to Merritt and a junction with the route already described. The main road from Calgary to Vancouver will have a total length of about six hundred miles, and will provide one of the most magnificent scenic routes in the world.

From Grande Prairie a branch is projected to Kamloops, and south to Nicola. By way of Kamloops and Ashcroft, also, connection may eventually be made with the famous Caribou Road to the north country, and in the far north, the Caribou Road may be extended to Fort George and up the Fraser to Robson and Jasper Parks, bringing the traveller back to the eastern side of the Rockies at Edmonton. From Kamloops, again, a road may be built up the North Thompson to Robson Park.

Another alternative route, and one that has already been practically decided upon, will swing east from Wardner and traverse the Crow's Nest Pass to the Alberta side of the mountains, where it will follow the foothills to Calgary. Still another branch of the main motor road will run from Castle Mountain through Rocky Mountains and Yoho Parks to Field and Golden, thence up the Columbia Valley to a junction with the main road. Portions of this branch road have already been built by the Dominion Government in the two parks. Apart from other advantages, the completion of this branch and of that portion of the main road from Castle Mountain to the Columbia Valley, will provide a motor road with easy grades through beautiful valleys and over several mountain passes, completely encircling the famous region of magnificent peaks, snow-fields, glaciers, lakes and waterfalls centring in Lake Louise, a region which in its combination of majesty and beauty, and its variety of colouring and composition, is surely without a peer. From the main road trails will lead inward to Consolation Valley, Moraine Lake and the Valley of the Ten Peaks, Paradise Valley, Lake O'Hara, the Ottertail Range, and a perfect galaxy of great peaks many of which have never yet been climbed or even visited.

As already mentioned, the administration of the Canadian National Parks is designed to interfere as little as possible either with the natural features of the parks or with the liberty of those who come to enjoy their beauty. There are in fact only two important MUST NOTS addressed to visitors in the Parks, and these are that they must not destroy trees, and that they must not kill wild animals. Even in these cases the policy is rather one of education than prohibition. People are being taught to appreciate the scenic as well as material value of the forest areas in the parks, and the simple precautions that are necessary to protect these areas from destruction by fire; and they are also learning to protect rather than destroy the wild life that seeks sanctuary here. One suggestion only remains of police supervision. If you bring a gun into any of the National Parks, it is sealed as you cross the boundary, and severe penalties are provided for breaking the seal while the sportsman remains within the park.

The marvellous effect of protected areas on the increase of wild life has been often commented upon, but the instinct which seems to draw all wild creatures, and particularly the more timid and shy animals, to these sanctuaries must always be a matter of interest and astonishment to visitors. To one who has watched the rapid increase in Rocky Mountains Park and the other reservations of animals which a few years ago were rarely seen, the situation is exceedingly gratifying. The diaries of park officers in this regard make interesting reading. Deer are now found everywhere in the park, and have become so tame that "numbers wandered into Banff town and remained there for days." Mountain goat are constantly met with along the trails, and were lately found on the east side of the Spray River, which had not occurred for many years. Flocks of twenty-five or more may be seen any day along the Banff-Laggan road. What is even more satisfactory, big-horn which had entirely disappeared from most parts of the Canadian Rockies are now increasing rapidly in the Parks. Black bear have become numerous, and a number of grizzlies and cubs have been seen, as well as red fox, wolverine, marten and lynx, and tracks of mountain lion. Large flocks of wild duck are reported on Bow Lake, as well as ruffled grouse, partridge, rabbits and other small game in the woods. Cinnamon bear are reported in Jasper Park, as well as a marked increase of beaver.

J. F. Porter

THE WALL OF JERICHO

John Woodruff

HOODOOS IN THE VALLEY OF THE BOW

A word or two may not be out of place as to some of the plans for the future of the Parks administration. The Zoo at Banff is to be moved to a much more suitable location on the lower slopes of Tunnel Mountain, and systematically developed with the object of making it a complete exhibition of the wild life of Western Canada. A special reserve is to be set apart in some suitable place for antelope, which do not appear to thrive in any of the existing parks. It is proposed to establish a protected area in the Fort Smith country about seven hundred miles north of Edmonton, for the preservation of the herd of wood buffalo—the only buffalo still living in the wild state. This would also be used as a sanctuary for other animals of the northern regions. It is also proposed, following the very successful experiments in Alaska, to provide reservations for reindeer in the Yukon. Another suggestion, which it is earnestly hoped may be adopted, looks to the setting apart at various points throughout the Dominion of small sanctuaries for the preservation of bird life.

One other plan that is being earnestly advocated by the progressive Commissioner of Dominion Parks will appeal with peculiar force to those who are labouring to bring the physical, mental and moral advantages of out-of-door life within reach of the masses of our city-dwellers. The plan is simply to bring National Parks to the people—a step distinctly in advance of the old policy of providing parks, and letting the people get to them if they were able. The Commissioner recognises the fact that the great mountain parks of Canada are for the most part accessible only to the comparatively well-to-do. To the majority of those who live in the cities the cost of the railway journey is of course prohibitive. He proposes, then, that the Dominion Government should secure a suitable tract of wild land within easy reach of each of the principal centres of population throughout the country, make it accessible by means of roads and trails, put it in charge of competent wardens, make it a sanctuary for the wild life of the neighbourhood, and throw it wide open to the people. Probably no other country is so favourably situated for such a measure at the present time. Wild land, with every variety of delightful natural scenery, may still be set apart or secured at no great cost within an hour or so's journey of most of the Canadian cities. At the same time these cities are growing at a phenomenal rate, and in a few years' time when the need of these natural playgrounds of the people will be much more acute than it is to-day, the cost of the land would probably be prohibitive. An illustration of what may be done for other Canadian cities is the proposed park on the British Columbia coast between Burrard Inlet and Pitt River. This park will be of great benefit to the present people of the city of Vancouver, but it will be of infinitely greater moment to the Vancouver of fifty years hence with its population of a million or more.

It is worth while to read the debates in the Canadian House of Commons of a quarter of a century ago, when the first of Canada's National Parks was set apart for the benefit of the people of the Dominion, and note the practical unanimity of sentiment among statesmen on both sides of politics, Sir John Macdonald, Sir Richard Cartwright, the late Lord Strathcona, Peter Mitchell, and many others, most of whom have since gone beyond the reach of worldly problems, as to the manifold advantages of such a policy. Equally significant are the words of the present Governor General, His Royal Highness the Duke of Connaught, at a meeting in Ottawa in March, 1913. "I do not think," he said, "that Canada realises what an asset the nation possesses in the parks. These areas have been preserved from the vandal hand of the builder for the use and enjoyment of the people, who may take their holidays there and keep close to nature under the most comfortable conditions, assuring a store of health which will make them the better able to cope with the strenuous life to which they return after their vacation."

Even more significant are the words of Lord Bryce, late ambassador to the United States: "Let us think of the future. We are the trustees of the future. We are not here for ourselves alone. All these gifts were not given to us to be used by one generation or with the thought of one generation only before our minds. We are the heirs of those who have gone before, and charged with the duty of what we owe to those who come after, and there is no duty which seems to be higher than that of handing on to them undiminished facilities for the enjoyment of some of the best gifts the Creator has seen fit to bestow upon His people."

III

IN AND ABOUT BANFF

BANFF is probably one of the most cosmopolitan communities in the world. Although its permanent population hardly exceeds one thousand, about 75,000 visitors registered during the season of 1913, coming from every out-of-the-way corner of the globe, Finland and Tasmania, the Isle of Man and the Fiji Islands, Siam, Korea and Japan, Norway, Egypt and the Argentine, New Zealand, Mexico, Turkey and Borneo. In fact, one is rather surprised to find no representative here from Greenland or Terra del Fuego. The bulk of these tourists of course come from other parts of Canada, from the United States, and from the United Kingdom, but practically every country in the world sends its quota, large or small, to this wonderful playground in the heart of the Canadian Rockies.

To accommodate all these visitors there are several comfortable hotels in Banff, notably the Banff Springs Hotel, and the Chateau Rundle. The Banff Springs Hotel, which has been repeatedly enlarged to meet the ever-increasing requirements of tourist traffic, stands on the summit of a rocky butte above the junction of the Bow and Spray Rivers, and commands a strikingly beautiful view to the eastward where the Bow has forced a passage between Tunnel Mountain and Mount Rundle. Bow Falls lie immediately beneath, and in the distance the Fairholme Range makes a splendid background.

Of the large number of tourists who visit the Canadian Alps, the majority do not get very far away from Banff. The reason is perhaps not hard to seek. At Banff they find, without any particular effort, delightful views of mountain scenery, with all the comforts and luxuries of eastern pleasure resorts. Comparatively short carriage drives over good roads take them to a dozen points of interest in the immediate neighbourhood. One of the most popular of these is the Cave and Basin, a mile or so up the valley of the Bow, where one may enjoy a plunge into the clear green waters of the pool. Other springs, with a much higher temperature, boil out of the upper slope of Sulphur Mountain, flowing over a series of brilliantly coloured terraces into natural limestone pools. Here, as well as at the Basin, bath-houses have been provided with every appliance for those who seek health or merely pleasure. The drive up to the springs, through the pines, and with ever-widening views of the enchanting valley, is well worth while for its own sake.

A much finer view, however, is to be had from the summit of Tunnel Mountain. One may drive, ride, or if he prefers a little moderate exercise, walk to the summit. The southern face of Tunnel Mountain drops in a sheer precipice nearly a thousand feet to the valley of the Bow. Beyond rises the rugged bulk of Rundle, with the Goat Range in the distance, the Spray winding as a silver thread down the valley, the Bow sweeping down from the northwest, a noble circle of peaks filling the horizon to the northwest and north, the Vermilion Lakes sparkling in their emerald setting, and around to the northeast, a glimpse of Lake Minnewanka.

With a fishing rod, and any other congenial companion, an enjoyable canoe trip may be had to Vermilion Lakes. The way lies up the Bow to Echo Creek, and by this miniature waterway to the lakes. As an afternoon's paddle nothing more delightful could be imagined, and the fishing is excellent, but the really serious fisherman will prefer the longer trip to Lake Minnewanka where lake trout are to be had of fighting temper and phenomenal size. Fourteen fish of a total weight of forty-three pounds represented one day's catch of a couple of sportsmen in this lake; sixteen caught the following day weighed forty-eight pounds. These, however, were pygmies beside the gigantic trout landed by Dr. Seward Webb in 1899, which tipped the scales at forty-seven pounds. To silence the incredulous, this monster is still preserved in a glass case at the Minnewanka Chalet.

A drive of nine miles from Banff, skirting the base of Cascade Mountain, lands the traveller on the shores of Lake Minnewanka. On the way he may visit a herd of about 25 buffalo, and enjoy the view from the rustic bridge down into the Devil's Canyon. The lake is some sixteen miles in length, and one may explore it either in a boat or by chartering the launch provided by the Canadian Pacific Railway. It swings, in the shape of a great sickle, around the base of Mount Inglismaldie, whose dizzy precipices soar some thousands of feet into the sky, with the glorious pinnacles of Mount Peechee in the background.

Another delightful drive leads past the Cave and Basin and around the northern end of Sulphur Mountain to Sundance Canyon, a weird little gorge through which Sundance Creek rushes down to its junction with the Bow. The plateau above the gorge was at one time a favourite Indian camping ground, and the scene of the barbaric Sun Dance.

On the northern bank of the Bow, high up above the river, stand a number of those fantastic natural monuments called Hoodoos, an excellent view of which may be gained by taking the drive around the Loop to the foot of Mount Rundle.

So far we have been confined to points of interest at no great distance from the village of Banff, and reached in each case by well-built carriage roads. Back and forth over these roads throughout the season drive streams of pilgrims, absorbing to a greater or less extent the manifold beauties of mountain, lake and river, wild canyon and sunny meadow, sombre pine woods and mountain slopes blazing with the rainbow colours of countless wildflowers; but above all, drinking in the glorious sunlight and revivifying air of the mountains. The great majority will always prefer to worship nature from the comfortable if somewhat crowded seat of a tally-ho, with a luxurious hotel to return to in the evening; and after all why should one blame them; but there will always be some who prefer the wild mountain trail to the macadamized road, the cayuse with all his idiosyncrasies to the upholstered coach, and the camp-fire to all the luxuries of a modern hotel.

THE VALLEY OF THE BOW

Fortunately there are to-day, and will be for some years to come, many miles of trail for each mile of road within the confines of the Canadian National Parks. The present policy seems to be to gradually develop the trails into carriage roads, but one may venture the hope that this policy will not be carried too far. The thought of driving to the foot of Mount Assiniboine on a motor bus, and having its glories profaned by a professional guide perhaps through a megaphone, is too painful to admit.

The evolution of mountain roads is an interesting problem in itself. The foundation is nearly always an Indian trail, one of those ancient thoroughfares that run hither and thither throughout the mountains, following the courses of innumerable streams, and winding up over mountain passes and down again to the valleys that lie beyond. There is a peculiar thrill of excitement in falling unexpectedly upon one of these relics of other days. The imagination leaps back to the time when Indian hunters followed them in search of elk and deer, mountain goat and bighorn. With the exception of a handful of Stonies, whose days are numbered, the Indian no longer hunts in the mountains; and the trails he once followed are now mostly covered with underbrush or blocked with fallen timber.

The first step in the conversion of an Indian trail into a modern road is to cut through the down timber. Expert axemen are sent out for this work, which varies according to circumstances from the cutting out of an occasional log to the hewing of a path through a tangle of fallen trees ten or fifteen feet high. Wherever possible the latter is of course left severely alone, but it sometimes happens that no way around the obstacle can be found and there is nothing for it but to cut out a path. The huge game of jack-straws may cover only a few yards, or it may extend for several miles.

Incidentally the axemen straighten the trail more or less. The practice among the Indians, and after them the fur-traders and white trappers, was to follow an old trail until a fallen tree blocked the way. It would have to be a formidable obstacle to stop the average cayuse, but occasionally even that professional acrobat was brought to a standstill. The rider in such case never cut his way through if it could be avoided. He followed the lines of least resistance, turned right or left through the standing timber until he had won around the fallen tree and back to the trail again. The next man took the new path, until he was perhaps brought up by a later windfall and in his turn added another twist to the devious course of the original trail. It can readily be imagined that these forest thoroughfares did not at any period of their history represent the shortest route between any two points; and it may as well be admitted here that the policy of every man for himself in trail-making is as active to-day as it was a hundred years ago. Each one of us who has camped in unfamiliar valleys of the mountains must plead guilty to the same selfish practice. Hurrying along the trail, anxious perhaps to reach a certain camping-ground before dark, the temptation to flank a fallen tree rather than laboriously cut through it, is irresistible. The thought is there, though we may not admit it, that we may never come this way again, and the next man must look out for himself.

It remains for the trail-makers to unravel the tangled skein and reduce it to something very remotely resembling a straight line. Having cut through the fallen timber and roughly bridged the deeper creeks, the result is a good pack trail. This is widened and cleared from year to year; levelled, graded and provided with substantial bridges, to convert it into a carriage road; and finally macadamized. And as the picturesque trail is converted into the eminently modern and respectable macadamized road, the equally picturesque pack-train disappears and in its place we see, and smell, that emblem of the twentieth century, the automobile.

However, let us not meet trouble half-way. There are still, thank fortune, many miles of trail in the Canadian national parks which the most enterprising automobile could not possibly negotiate, and many more miles of wonderful mountain country that as yet are even trailess. From the main road which follows the Bow River, and roughly speaking runs southeast and northwest through the centre of the Banff Park, good trails branch off on either side up every important valley. Portions of some of these have been converted into roads, such as those to Lake Minnewanka, Sundance Canyon and up Spray River. From the Chalet at the western end of Lake Minnewanka, where the road now ends, a trail has been opened along the north shore of the lake to its eastern extremity, through the Devil's Gap and Ghost Valley, and across the South Fork of Ghost River to the Stony Indian Reserve, which lies just outside the Park.

Ghost Valley is a weird, uncanny canyon, the scene of many wild Indian legends. It is believed to mark the ancient valley of the Bow, Minnewanka and a couple of smaller lakes being the sole remaining relics of the channel. No water now runs through Ghost Valley, though mountain torrents and waterfalls dash down its precipitous sides. Each disappears in its limestone bed, which must cover a network of subterranean channels. The mountains end abruptly in the Devil's Gap, from which one looks out on the plains, or rather on the border land between plain and mountain. A few miles to the north rises a grim peak known as the Devil's Head, and the whole country is studded with Hoodoos and other strange natural features appropriate to such a region.

Sir George Simpson, who entered the mountains by the Devil's Gap on his expedition of 1841, camped by the side of Lake Minnewanka, which he named Lake Peechee after his guide, a chief of the Mountain Crees. Peechee is still remembered in the splendid peak which rises behind Mount Inglismaldie. Ghost Valley was the scene of an exploit of which Sir George Simpson tells the story.

A Cree and his squaw had been tracked into the valley by five warriors of a hostile tribe. "On perceiving the odds that were against him, the man gave himself up for lost, observing to the woman that as they could die but once they had better make up their minds to submit to their present fate without resistance. The wife, however, replied that as they had but one life to lose, they were the more decidedly bound to defend it to the last, even under the most desperate circumstances; adding that, as they were young and by no means pitiful, they had an additional motive for preventing their hearts from becoming small. Then, suiting the action to the word, the heroine brought the foremost warrior to the earth with a bullet, while the husband, animated by a mixture of shame and hope, disposed of two more of the enemy with his arrows. The fourth, who had by this time come to pretty close quarters, was ready to take vengeance on the courageous woman with uplifted tomahawk, when he stumbled and fell; and in the twinkling of an eye the dagger of his intended victim was buried in his heart. Dismayed at the death of his four companions, the sole survivor of the assailing party saved himself by flight, after wounding his male opponent by a ball in the arm."

Canadian Pacific Railway Company

TRAIL NEAR BANFF

Other trails lead up Cascade River from the Minnewanka road, and over the Park boundaries to the Panther River country, connecting also at Sawback Creek with the Forty Mile trail; and up the east bank of Spray River, and between the Goat Range and the Three Sisters, to Trout Lakes, connecting with the road which follows the west bank of the Spray, and continuing on to the foot of Mount Assiniboine, just over the Park boundaries, which on this southwestern side follow the height of land. Another runs from the end of the Sundance Canyon road up Healy Creek to Simpson Pass, with a branch trail to Fatigue Mountain on the divide; while others again take you up Redearth Creek to Shadow Lake and one of the giants of this part of the Rockies, Mount Ball, and by way of Johnston Creek to the Sawback Range and its wonderful glaciers. It is impossible to give any real impression of the marvellous region through which these mountain trails lead you, of its scores of great peaks whose turrets, spires or domes climb into the very heavens, of its snow-fields and glaciers, bleak mountain passes and exquisite alpine meadows carpeted with millions of flowers, its primæval forests and rushing torrents, sparkling waterfalls and emerald or turquoise lakes. To appreciate the mountains, you must come and see them at first hand, and to see them at their very best, you must take tent and pony and provisions, not forgetting tobacco if you are a normal man, and get well out on the trail, away from hotels and railways and every suggestion of the artificial life you have left behind you.

IV

THE CANADIAN MATTERHORN

Mount Assiniboine lies about sixteen miles from Banff as the crow flies, but by trail it is more than twice that distance. It is not visible from any of the lower mountains about Banff, such as Tunnel and Sulphur, being hidden by the intervening ranges, but if you are sufficient of a mountain-climber to win to the summit of Mount Rundle you will gain a view of the mighty pyramid to the south that will alone make the climb worth while. Cascade Mountain, some miles north of the Bow, also offers the ambitious climber an inspiring sight of the Matterhorn of the Rockies. Sir James Outram, the famous mountaineer, who was the first man to reach the summit of Assiniboine, says that the view he had of the peak from the summit of Cascade Mountain, towering over two thousand feet above where he stood, first fired his ambition to conquer what was then believed to be an unscalable peak.

The first mention of Mount Assiniboine is in the report of the Rocky Mountain expedition of the late George M. Dawson, of the Canadian Geological Survey, in 1884. It is quite possible that the peak may have been seen by the missionary De Smet, who crossed the White Man's Pass in 1845, but he says nothing about it in his narrative. Dr. Dawson first saw the peak from Copper Mountain, some distance west of Banff, and later from White Man's Pass, near what is now the southern extremity of the Park. He named it after the tribe of Indians known as the Assiniboines.

But although Dr. Dawson and his party of surveyors saw and admired Mount Assiniboine from a distance, neither he nor any other white man is known to have reached its base until 1893, when R. L. Barrett, an American mountain-climber, with Tom Wilson of Banff, made their way to its foot by way of Healy Creek, Simpson Pass and Simpson River. Two years later Mr. Barrett made a second trip to the mountain by the same route, accompanied this time by James F. Porter and Walter Dwight Wilcox, who has since become widely known as an interpreter of Rocky Mountain scenery. Tom Wilson outfitted the party, but was unable to accompany them. He sent, however, one of his best men, Bill Peyto.

Mary M. Vaux, W. S. Vaux, and G. Vaux, Jr.

MOUNT ASSINIBOINE

(*The Matterhorn of the Rockies*)

Wilson, Peyto and Fred Stephens are *the* guides of the Canadian Rockies. There are to-day scores of more or less capable guides in the various National Parks, but these three alone are famous. One or other of them has accompanied, or led, nearly every expedition of any note into the unexplored parts of the mountains. Tom Wilson is not only a competent outfitter and a splendid guide, but he is also a renowned spinner of yarns, and a very mine of information on the Rockies. As some one has said of him, he knows more about the Canadian Rockies than any other man has ever yet possessed. A visit to Tom Wilson is not the least delightful of memories that the intelligent tourist will carry away with him from Banff. Stephens and Peyto are men of the same calibre, unerring on the trail, delightful around the camp-fire, and withal thoroughly good fellows. But we must leave them for the present, and return to the Assiniboine expedition.

The first camp was made on Healy Creek, where they arrived after a long tramp over a bad trail, soaked through from wet brush, but nevertheless thoroughly happy. The camp-fire soon dried their clothes, a hot supper was before them, and after that they would roll themselves up in their blankets and sleep as only those may sleep whose bed is of balsam boughs and who breathe the life-giving air of the mountains. Above all, they were on the road to Assiniboine.

The next day's journey took them up the north fork of Healy Creek, and they camped a few miles from Simpson Pass, crossing the continental divide from Alberta into British Columbia the following morning. At the summit the snow drifts were fifteen or twenty feet deep, though it was the month of July, but as they turned down the southerly slope the snow disappeared and in its place appeared immense banks of white anemones and yellow Alpine lilies. The mossy woods through which the trail led them the previous day had been carpeted with the round-leafed orchid, with here and there a nodding Calypso, one of the most daintily beautiful and fragrant of the mountain flowers.

On the northern side of the pass they had left behind a stream whose waters eventually flow into Hudson Bay. An Indian trail now led them through deep and sombre woods, beside the banks of a river which empties into the Pacific Ocean. The following day they travelled through the Simpson valley, crossing and recrossing the river or its small branches, and camping in a high valley two thousand feet above the river, above which again towered on either side smooth cliffs whose dark faces were relieved with silvery waterfalls. Opposite the camp the walls of the mountain had been carved by nature into one of those curiously realistic representations of a mediæval castle that is found here and there in the Rockies. "One might easily imagine that these sharp pinnacles and rocky clefts were ramparts, embrasures, and turreted fortifications. But the wild goats, marmots and picas were the sole owners of this castle."

A few hours' tramp brought them the next day to the summit of a high pass, from which they had their first glimpse of Assiniboine, piercing the sky beyond an intervening barrier of snowy peaks. Another day's journey, through fallen timber, along the winding shore of a beautiful lake, and over a rocky ridge to a second lake, brought them to the object of their heart's desire. Assiniboine at last!

EMPEROR FALLS

R. C. W. Lett

"The majestic mountain," says Wilcox, "which is a noble pyramid of rock towering above snow fields, was clearly reflected in the water surface. Such a picture so suddenly revealed aroused the utmost enthusiasm of all our party, and unconsciously every one paused in admiration while our horses strayed from the trail to graze. Continuing once more, we traversed some open places among low ridges covered with beautiful larches. We passed through a delightful region which descended gently for half a mile to a treeless moor, where we pitched camp. Behind us was a clump of trees, before us Mount Assiniboine, and on our left a lake of considerable size, which washed the very base of the mountain and extended northwards in the bottom of a broad valley."

Here they remained for a couple of weeks, exploring the neighbourhood, and obtaining photographs of the mountain, some of which are reproduced in Wilcox's wonderfully illustrated book on the Rockies. A couple of days were spent by Wilcox, Barrett and Peyto in a complete circuit of the mountain, a distance as they were compelled to travel of fifty-one miles, through a country for the most part absolutely devoid of trails, and covered in places with a very wilderness of fallen timber. For hours their only means of travel was along the tops of prostrate trunks piled ten and twelve feet above the ground. They were rewarded, however, by a magnificent view of the south side of Mount Assiniboine, never before revealed to white men.

The fascination of this singularly noble peak and its splendid setting of névé and glacier, lake and forest, drew Mr. Wilcox to its feet again in 1899, accompanied this time by Henry G. Bryant and Louis J. Steele, who made the first attempt to climb the mountain, reaching an elevation of ten thousand feet. Approaching storms then drove them back, and on the last ice slope they both had a narrow escape. Steele lost his foothold and dragged Bryant with him. "There was but one possible escape from a terrible fall. A projecting rock of considerable size appeared not far below, and Steele with a skilful lunge of his ice-axe swung round to it and anchored himself in a narrow crevice where the snow had melted away. No sooner had he come to a stop than Bryant shot over him from above and likewise found safety. Otherwise they would have fallen about six hundred feet, with serious if not fatal results."

An incident of the outward journey is so characteristic of one of the innumerable phases of Rocky Mountain scenery that one may venture to borrow Mr. Wilcox's graphic description: "Whatever interest there may have been to learn our whereabouts was absorbed upon reaching the ridge crest by a revelation of wild and gloomy grandeur that I have never seen equalled. Our little band of men and horses were standing upon a craggy ledge, where splintered rocks, frost-rent and rough, rose through perpetual snows, making a tower of observation, whence we looked out upon a mountain wilderness. Shifting winds were sweeping fog-banks and clouds far above the highest trees of a forest-clad valley, not faintly discernible through the storm. Yet they were below the crest of our lofty pinnacle, where our storm-beaten band of horses, steaming in moisture, stood darkly outlined against the pale mists. No gleam of light broke through the lurid sky. The monotonous grey of falling snow had given place to heaving bands of clouds, for the storm was breaking. Then slowly and mysteriously beyond a dark abyss rose a beautiful vision of mountains clad in new snow. Their bases rested on unsubstantial fog, their tops were partially concealed by clinging mists, and they were apparently so far away as to seem like the highest mountains in the world."

Their route to the mountain from Banff had been by a branch of Healy Creek to the continental divide and along this high plateau to Simpson valley; they returned by way of the Spray. This is now the recognised route to Assiniboine, along which the Park authorities have opened a good trail. Mr. Wilcox describes it as the easiest, and at the same time most uninteresting, of several possible routes; and that by way of Healy Creek and the continental divide as the most varied and attractive. A good trail is now available up Healy Creek to the plateau, and no doubt in time it will be extended to Mount Assiniboine. Another shorter route by the south fork of Healy Creek has also been partially opened; so that in the course of a year or two it will be possible to visit the monarch of the southern Canadian Rockies by any one of several alternative routes.

Although popularly reputed to be unscalable, attempts were made after that of Bryant and Steele to get to the summit of Mount Assiniboine, first by two brothers named Walling, and later by Bryant and Wilcox, but without success although the first record of ten thousand feet was considerably increased. Finally, however, in 1901, Mr. (now Sir James) Outram, with two Swiss guides, Häsler and Bohren, reached the highest peak after six hours' climbing. The story of the climb is modestly told in Outram's book, the following passages from which will give some idea at least of the stupendous precipices that had to be negotiated and the skill and daring demanded in such a climb. On the way up Outram rested for a time near the summit of one of the spurs of the main peak. "Here," he says, "for some moments I stood in solemn awe, perched like a statue in a lofty niche cut in the topmost angle of a vast, titanic temple, with space in front, on either side, above, below, the yawning depths lost in the wreathing mists that wrapped the mountain's base."

After a perilous ascent where nerve, sure-footedness, and quick judgment were needed every moment, they finally reached the summit of the mountain. "One at a time—the other two securely anchored—we crawled with the utmost caution to the actual highest point (an immense snow cornice) and peeped over the edge of the huge, overhanging crest, down the sheer wall to a great shining glacier 6000 feet or more below.... Perched high upon our isolated pinnacle, fully 1500 feet above the loftiest peak for many miles around, below us lay unfolded range after range of brown-grey mountains, patched with snow and some times glacier hung, intersected by deep chasms or broader wooded valleys. A dozen lakes were counted, nestling between the outlying ridges of our peak, which supply the head-waters of three rivers—the Cross, the Simpson and the Spray."

After resting on the summit, it was decided to descend by another and even more difficult route—one in fact that had hitherto been thought impossible. Outram had studied it from below, however, and was confident that it could be negotiated.

"Well roped," he writes, "and moving generally one at a time, we clambered downward foot by foot, now balancing upon the narrow ledge, 5000 feet of space at our right hand; then scrambling down a broken wall-end, the rocks so friable that handhold after handhold had to be abandoned, and often half a dozen tested before a safe one could be found; now, when the ridge became too jagged or too sheer, making our cautious way along a tiny ledge or down the face itself, clinging to the cold buttresses, our fingers tightly clutching the scant projection of some icy knob, or digging into small interstices between the rocks; anon, an ice-slope had to be negotiated with laborious cutting of steps in the hard wall-like surface; and again, cliff after cliff must be reconnoitred, its slippery upper rim traversed until a cleft was found and a gymnastic descent effected to the ice-bound declivity that fell away beneath its base.

A. Knechtel

MOUNT EDITH

"For close upon 2000 feet the utmost skill and care were imperative at every step; for scarcely half a dozen could be taken in that distance where an unroped man who slipped would not inevitably have followed the rejected handholds and débris, that hurtled down in leaps and bounds to crash in fragments on the rocks and boulders far below."

Beside this daring climb down the steep north arête of Assiniboine may be placed an even more perilous incident of the descent of Mount Bryce the following year. Outram had made the ascent with the Swiss guide Christian Kaufmann, taking eleven hours to reach the summit. With a long and difficult climb down the mountain in prospect, and a particularly dangerous cliff to be negotiated, which had been troublesome enough on the way up and would be much more dangerous now, they spent very little time on the summit.

A. O. Wheeler

TOWERS OF MOUNT BABEL

(Consolation Valley)

"It was almost dark," says Outram, "when we approached the well remembered cliff, which had been continually on our minds, and to reach which before nightfall had been the object of our hasty, foodless march. But we arrived too late. And now the question arose as to the wisest course to take. We were on the horns of a dilemma. To go on meant descending practically in the dark a cliff which we had deemed so difficult by daylight as almost to be deterred from undertaking it at all. But on the other hand, a night out 10,000 feet above the sea, without the smallest vestige of shelter, on the exposed sky-line of a ridge swept by an arctic wind, with boots and stockings saturated and certain to freeze (and possibly the feet inside as well) before the dawn could aid us on our way, and almost destitute of food, offered a prospect particularly uninviting. I left the decision to Kaufmann. The risk was practically his alone. For me, descending first with the good rope in his trusty grasp, there was no danger, even should I slip or fail to find a hold, except for the short distance where both would be upon the face at the same time. For him, a slip, a lost grip or a broken hold might mean destruction. But he voted for advance, and at any rate I could make a trial and report upon my personal sensations before his turn arrived. So I turned my face towards the rock, slipped over the edge, and entered on the fateful climb.

"It will be long before I lose the recollection of those seventy feet of cliff. Drawn out for one long hour of concentrated tension were the successive experiences of hopeless groping in the dark depths for something to rest a foot upon, of blind search all over the chilled rocky surface for a knob or tiny crack where the numbed fingers might find another hold, of agonizing doubt as to their stability when found, of eerie thrill and sickening sensation when the long-sought support crumbled beneath the stress and hurtled downward into the blackness of space, whilst the hollow reverberations of its fall re-echoed through the silence. Then the strain of waiting on the best, but very questionable, protuberances for several tense minutes of motionless suspense, whilst the exigencies of the rope compelled Christian to climb down fifteen or twenty feet, and I could move again. At long last came the marvellous relief of feeling solid and sufficient standing-room once more, followed by the still more trying period of inactivity, the patient intensity of watching and hauling in the slack as the rope came slowly and spasmodically down, telling of Christian's gradual descent, the strained anxiety lest any accident should happen to my comrade, and, finally, the thankfulness of seeing his figure looming close above and in a few moments standing by my side, and we could breathe again."

V

INCOMPARABLE LAKE LOUISE

T HIRTY-FIVE miles west of Banff on the Canadian Pacific Railway, and still in the Rocky Mountains Park, is the village of Laggan. You may make the journey by train or motor, in either case enjoying a succession of magnificent views of mountain peaks on either side, culminating in the majestic Mount Temple. From Laggan a tramway or a somewhat dusty ride or drive of two or three miles up the mountain side brings you to the Chalet, on the shores of Lake Louise; but if you are wise you will take the woodland trail and walk. The trail winds up through the woods, cool and fragrant, with wildflowers about you on every side, charming glimpses of forest glades and mountain torrents, and far above the æolian music of the breeze in the tree tops. The trail ends at the Chalet, a rambling, picturesque, and thoroughly comfortable hotel, crowded with tourists from the ends of the earth. Your thoughts are not, however, of hotel or tourists as you look beyond the trees, and get your first vivid impression of what is probably the most perfect bit of scenery in the known world. A lake of the deepest and most exquisite colouring, ever changing, defying analysis, mirroring in its wonderful depths the sombre forests and cliffs that rise from its shores on either side, the gleaming white glacier and tremendous, snow-crowned peaks that fill the background of the picture, and the blue sky and fleecy cloud overhead. Year after year you may revisit Lake Louise, and wander about its shores through all kinds of weather; you will never exhaust the variety of its charms. It changes from day to day, from hour to hour, from moment to moment. It responds instantly to every subtle change of cloud, wind or atmosphere; it has one glory of the sunrise and another of sunset; it offers you one picture under the brilliant noonday sun, another under heavy clouds, another through driving mists, or rain, or snow; but always incomparably beautiful, and always indescribable.

Let us see how it has appealed to different men, who have visited it at different times and under varied conditions. As long ago as 1888 William Spotswood Green, of the British Alpine Club, climbed up to the shores of Lake Louise on his way back from a season's mountain-climbing in the Selkirks. "I was," he says, "quite unprepared for the full beauty of the scene. Nothing of the kind could possibly surpass it. I was somewhat reminded of the Oeschinen See in Switzerland, but Lake Louise is about twice as long, the forests surrounding it are far richer, and the grouping of the mountains is simply perfection."

Canadian Pacific Railway Company

PARADISE VALLEY

(From the Saddleback)

"Lake Louise," says Walter Dwight Wilcox, "is a realisation of the perfect beauty of nature beyond the power of imagination."

Sir James Outram quotes the final verdict of one whom he describes as "a close observer of nature and enthusiastic lover of the picturesque," to this effect: "I have travelled in almost every country under heaven, yet I have never seen so perfect a picture in the vast gallery of Nature's masterpieces." And Outram himself writes:

"As a gem of composition and of colouring it is perhaps unrivalled anywhere. To those who have not seen it words must fail to conjure up the glories of that 'Haunted Lake among the pine-clad mountains, forever smiling upward to the skies.' A master's hand indeed has painted all its beauties; the turquoise surface, quivering with fleeting ripples, beyond the flower-strewn sweep of grassy shore; the darkening mass of tapering spruce and pine trees, mantling heavily the swiftly rising slopes that culminate in rugged steeps and beetling precipices, soaring aloft into the sun-kissed air on either side; and there, beyond the painted portals of the narrowing valley, rich with the hues of royal purple and of sunset reds, the enraptured gaze is lifted to a climax of superb effects, and the black walls of Mount Lefroy, surrounded by their dazzling canopy of hanging glaciers, and the wide gable-sweep of Mount Victoria, resplendent with its spotless covering of eternal snow, crown the matchless scene. The azure dome of heaven, flecked with bright, fleecy clouds like angel's wings, completes the picture."

Canadian Pacific Railway Company

GIANT STEPS

(Head of Paradise Valley)

Tom Wilson seems to have been the first white man to visit the shores of Lake Louise. At least his is the first visit of which there is any record. According to Wilcox, he camped with a pack train near the mouth of the Pipestone in 1882, when some Stony Indians came along and placed their tepees near him. "Not long after, a heavy snow-slide or avalanche was heard among the mountains to the south, and in reply to inquiry one of the Indians named Edwin, the Gold Seeker, said that the thunder came from a 'big snow mountain above the lake of little fishes'. The next day Wilson and Edwin rode through the forests to the lake of little fishes, which was named subsequently for the Princess Louise," then in Canada as the wife of the Governor General, the late Duke of Argyll.

G. and W. Fear

LAKE LOUISE

Professor A. P. Coleman, of Toronto University, who has spent many summers in the Canadian Rockies, and to whom we are indebted for one of the most comprehensive and entertaining narratives of exploration in this fascinating field, visited Lake Louise two years after Tom Wilson. "I scrambled along its shores," he says, "then unnamed and without marks of human habitation where the comfortable chalet now rises." Many of us would give a good deal to treasure in our memory a picture of Lake Louise sans chalet and sans tourists.

About a quarter of a century ago the Canadian Pacific Railway built an unpretentious log inn on the shores of the lake, with accommodation for a few guests. This was destroyed by fire in 1893. It was rebuilt the following year, and has been repeatedly enlarged to meet the demands of an ever-growing stream of tourists, the last addition costing somewhere in the neighbourhood of half a million dollars. The railway has also provided a good road and trail from Laggan up to the Chalet, and opened several trails to points of interest about the lake. These have since been improved and extended in every direction by the Canadian government.

It is doubtful if any other spot in the mountains accommodates itself so generously to all tastes and capacities as does Lake Louise. If you are hopelessly indolent, you may stroll down to the shore, over a carpet of wildflowers, and lazily enjoy the matchless picture of Lefroy and Victoria with the gem of a lake in the foreground. Or a half-mile's walk along the excellent trail that skirts the right-hand side of the lake will prove a revelation of ever-changing and always superb views. The walk may be extended to the farther end of the lake, and back by the other side where the path climbs along the steep slope of Fairview Mountain. An alternative trip, and a particularly delightful one in the early morning or the evening twilight, is to take one of the boats at the Chalet and row to the end of the lake and back. The distance is extraordinarily deceptive. It looks but a stone's-throw, yet when you have rowed three-quarters of a mile you find that you are not much more than half-way. You look up on either side to the towering cliffs, and feel like a water beetle in the bottom of a gigantic cup. And what a wonderful liquid is contained in this cup; so clear that you grow dizzy as you gaze down and down into its unfathomable depths, and so marvellously steeped in colour that it is impossible to believe as you dip into it that your hand will not come up the same deep turquoise.

From the end of the lake a trail leads to the foot of Victoria Glacier, opening up an ever-changing panorama of dazzling snow-fields and terrific precipices. This way lies the road of the experienced mountaineers who with skill and daring win their way to the summits of these giants far up amid the clouds. It was by this road and the Lefroy Glacier that Wilcox some years ago unexpectedly discovered Paradise Valley.

A good trail now leads from the Chalet around Saddle Mountain to Paradise Valley, but one of the finest views of the valley with dainty Lake Annette and the gigantic guardian peaks that tower above, Temple, Aberdeen, Sheol and the Mitre, can be obtained from Saddle Mountain, reached by an easy trail. One does not readily forget the exquisite view that rewards the climber as he reaches the summit of the Saddle and stands on the edge of a thousand-foot precipice that drops sheer to the valley, and yet seems insignificant when the eye goes up and up to the glittering peak of Temple Mountain soaring thousands of feet above. The very contrast of the frowning walls that shut it in on every side lends an additional charm to the fairyland that lies at their feet, a perfect picture of green meadows, blue lake and silvery streams, most appropriately named Paradise Valley.

From the Saddle a zigzag trail leads to the summit of Fairview Mountain, from which one may look down upon Lake Louise whose ever-shifting shades of blue and green seem even deeper and richer than seen from the shore.

Mary M. Vaux, W. S. Vaux, and G. Vaux, Jr.

MORAINE LAKE

From the Chalet again a ride or climb up the trail that branches off on the right-hand side of the lake brings one to Mirror Lake and Lake Agnes. The distance to the former is about two miles, and a little more to Lake Agnes. Mirror Lake lies at the foot of a curious rock called the Beehive, and Lake Agnes is reached by a short climb up the slope of the mountain. The lakes themselves are well worth the climb, but one is rewarded as well with entirely new views of the encircling peaks, and tramps through a bewildering garden of Alpine flowers among which one finds the antennaria and bryanthus, which so curiously resemble edelweiss and purple heather.

A short distance north of Lake Agnes is the Little Beehive, a mere knob on the mountain, from which, however, a magnificent view is obtained of a far-flung panorama of tremendous, snow-clad mountains, blue lakes, green forest slopes and sparkling glaciers. "I have never," says Wilcox, "seen this glorious ensemble of forests, lakes and snow fields surpassed in an experience on the summits of more than forty peaks and the middle slopes of as many more in the Canadian Rockies." And, as he adds, the viewpoint is accessible to even the most indifferent climbers, or may be managed on horseback.

From the Chalet, also, a trail of ten miles leads to the Valley of the Ten Peaks and Moraine Lake, or the valley may be reached by a carriage road which extends to the foot of the lake. Another trail runs from Moraine Lake around an imposing cliff known as the Tower of Babel to Consolation Valley, and still another leads in the opposite direction to Wenkchemna Glacier.

A somewhat longer expedition from Lake Louise is by trail west to the height of land at Stephen, then down the picturesque Valley of the Kicking Horse, and up Cataract Creek on the western side of Mount Victoria, to Lake O'Hara. This, however, takes one into Yoho Park, of which something will be said in the next chapter.

VI

THE VALLEY OF THE YOHO

TRAVELLING west on the main line of the Canadian Pacific Railway, we cross the continental divide at or near Stephen. The actual summit is marked by a rustic arch. From the steep mountainside comes a little stream which branches above; the two branches flow through the arch and then separate, one bound for the Pacific the other for the Atlantic.

This arch marks not only the height of land but also the boundary between Rocky Mountains Park and Yoho Park, the former in the Province of Alberta, the latter in British Columbia. An hour's run brings us to the headquarters of Yoho Park at Field, with Mount Stephen's massive dome far above, six thousand four hundred feet from where we stand.

With Field as a starting-point we can reach by road or trail all the principal points of interest in the park, the Kicking Horse Canyon and the Natural Bridge, Mount Stephen and the famous fossil beds, Emerald Lake, the Amiskwi Valley, Lake O'Hara, Lake Oesa and Lake McArthur, and the wonderful valley from which the park takes its name, with its exquisitely beautiful waterfalls.

At Field, as at Banff in Rocky Mountains Park and Glacier in Glacier Park, a number of Swiss guides are stationed throughout the season, for the benefit of those who enjoy the pleasures of mountain-climbing. Mount Stephen, on account of its accessibility and the magnificent views that reward the mountaineer, is the most climbed peak in the Canadian Rockies. Unlike some of its huge neighbours, such as Cathedral Mountain, Lefroy, Deltaform, Hungabee and Goodsir, it is within the capacity of any reasonably energetic man or woman, with or without experience in mountain-climbing, provided one has the assistance of a competent guide.

In the autumn of 1904 Mount Stephen was climbed under conditions that could not be recommended to any but the most expert and clearheaded of mountain-climbers. Rev. George Kinney was then at Field, and had gone for a solitary ramble to the fossil beds on Mount Stephen. After several hours spent in gathering trilobites he ate his lunch, and then the desire seized him to get some pictures from the summit of the mountain. Shouldering his two cameras he set out to climb the peak.

Mary M. Vaux, W. S. Vaux, and G. Vaux, Jr.

TAKAKKAW FALLS

(Yoho Valley)

"It only took a few minutes," he says, "to climb to the top of the spur immediately above the fossil bed and to get above the last of the struggling timber growth, when there burst into view a scene that beggars description: Cathedral Mountain, its perpendicular heights searching the very heavens, formed one unbroken wall of a vast amphitheatre. There, ridge on ridge, tier on tier, the parallel ledges, cushioned with snow, rose in countless numbers for thousands of feet. In such places as these the spirits of the mountain sit and watch the changing scenes of the hills in the vast arena before them. Sometimes it is a procession of sheep, or goats, or deer, or bear, or the eagle gracefully sailing. Sometimes it is the frisking mountain rat, or the whistling marmot, or the busy haymaker curing his crops of hay on the hot rocks of the slide. Or again it is the grand orchestra of the hills, breaking forth in the roar of the avalanche, the scream of the wind, the fall of the cataract, or the crumbling of the peaks.

"For a mile or more it was easy going over a gentle slope covered with rocks and snow. The clouds had gradually broken up before the genial warmth of the sun, and the Kicking Horse River seemed a little thread of silver that wound, with countless twists and turns, in a level valley below. Field, with its roundhouses and trains and big hotel seemed but a little dot, and when an engine whistled a thousand echoes tossed the sound from side to side, from peak to peak, from canyon to canyon, until it was lost in immensity.

"The climb was uneventful up to the time the cliffs near the top were reached. It had been a fairly easy slope all the way. The snow began at timber line, and was hard enough to walk on its top. Mount Dennis was slowly left behind and sank to a mere hillock beneath. Mounts Field and Burgess gradually slipped down until Wapta and then the Vice-President, with an emerald glacier in its lap, came in full view from behind.

"By making a detour I could have found an easier way, but, having no guide and never having been there before, I began to climb the wall of rock immediately in front. It was a most difficult climb. The short day was nearly ended, the warmth of the sun had given place to a raw, cold wind, and my pack being large and heavy got in the way. Nearing the top of this almost vertical cliff my numb fingers slipped and I barely escaped a sheer fall of fully one hundred feet. Surmounting the cliff, it proved but a vanguard of many. Height on height of barefaced cliffs offered their resistance in succession, each crowned with snow-covered ledges. Gradually, however, they were vanquished, one by one, and at last I stood on the glory-crowned summit, ten thousand five hundred feet above the sea.

"Mounts Field, Burgess and Wapta lay far beneath. President and Vice-President gleamed and glistened in the near distance. Cathedral Mountain, close by, seemed almost on a level. Here, there, everywhere, some in groups, others in serried ranks, were massed the war-scarred veterans of an innumerable host—the rugged remnants of a vast ancient plateau stretching north, southeast and west, as far as the eye could see. All this vast array of snow-clad peaks, frowning precipices, glistening glaciers, and yawning gulfs was burnished with the glowing hues of the setting sun. I watched him sink behind the distant fringe of peaks in the west, and when he was gone how lonely and chill those sombre old masses seemed. I shouted aloud, but my voice was immediately swallowed up in that awful still-ness, for there was nothing to give it an echo.

Mary M. Vaux, W. S. Vaux, and G. Vaux, Jr.

LAKE O'HARA

(Yoho Park)

"I did not stay long on the summit, for the raw, cold winds that had frozen the snow in crystals several inches long chilled one to the bone. The darkness of night began to swallow up the distant hills, and it was necessary to get down the cliffs while there was still light to see the way. I had gone but a short distance when, following a ledge around more to the south, I made a grand discovery. There, filling a steep, rugged ravine that seemed to extend all the way to Cathedral Mountain was a smooth pathway of snow, steep as the roof of a house. One question flashed to my mind: would it be frozen too hard? I cautiously tried it. Yes! it was hard, but with care it could be travelled. By launching out freely and letting the whole weight come down on each foot at a time, the heels could be forced a couple of inches into the solid snow. Here, indeed, was the best kind of speedy going: swing out one foot, spring from the other, and land on the heel in an inch or two of snow. Each stride covered a distance of several feet, and it was possible to run down that steep precipice of snow as fast as I liked, but my life depended on each heel getting that little two inches of a hold; one slip would mean a fearful slide to death. There was no danger of crevices, for it was all new snow.

"In an amazingly short time a descent of hundreds of feet had been made, until finally the bottom of the cliffs was reached. Then I started across and down that long, tedious slope of snow and boulders." Finally he regained the fossil beds, picked up his belongings, and made his way back to Field in the dark.

To climb Mount Stephen alone, and in October, is a feat that would be considered foolhardy by any mountaineer less capable and sure-headed than George Kinney. Mr. Kinney has since proved his mettle on a much more formidable climb, to the summit of the monarch of the Canadian Rockies, Mount Robson. This, however, will stand for a later chapter.

The road from Stephen, or Hector, down to Field is an exceedingly interesting one, and worth taking in as leisurely a manner as possible, on an easy-going pony, or better still on foot. Leaving Hector, the road skirts the shores of Wapta Lake, whose waters are of the deepest blue; Cataract Creek trail here leads off to the south, to Lake O'Hara about eight miles distant beyond the great white peak of Mount Victoria; the Cathedral Crags lie directly ahead to the west, and beneath winds the wildly impressive Canyon of the Kicking Horse. As the road drops rapidly down the valley, one is lost in amazement at the temerity of the engineers who dared to carry a railway through this seemingly impossible gorge, with its gradient of nearly 200 feet in the mile. As we leave the Canyon behind, Mount Stephen fills the view ahead, with Field and Wapta to the right, and the beautiful Yoho Valley opening up to the north, where the Wapta icefield and Mount Habel are visible in the distance.

One of the most delightful expeditions in Yoho Park is that to Lake O'Hara and Lake McArthur. These may be reached either from Laggan in Rocky Mountains Park, or from Field in the Yoho. Outram recommends that if at all possible the approach should be made from Laggan and Lake Louise, by way of Abbot Pass, using the easier but less picturesque Cataract trail for the return journey. This makes a somewhat strenuous trip for those who may not be accustomed to climbing, but otherwise is thoroughly worth the extra effort. The way leads around Lake Louise, and over the Victoria Glacier to Abbot Pass, with the tremendous precipices of Lefroy and Victoria frowning down on either side. From the glacier the way to the pass is up a steep, narrow gorge known as the Death Trap on account of the numerous avalanches that hurtle down from the mountain tops. The danger, however, is more apparent than real, and nothing has ever happened to justify the sinister name.

From the summit of the pass the view is one of indescribable grandeur, a wilderness of gigantic cliffs far and near, stretching up and up to glittering summits. Scrambling down the steep descent, Lake Oesa comes into view far below, at the foot of Mount Yukness. Oesa is an Indian word meaning Ice, and the lake has been appropriately named as, on account of its elevation, it is frozen over throughout the greater part of the year and never quite free from ice. A climb down ledges and talus slopes brings one to the little lake, and from here the first glimpse is caught of the exquisitely beautiful Lake O'Hara in the valley far below. As one gets nearer, the loveliness of this secluded lake grows, and is all the more compelling because of the absolute stillness, no chalet or carriages or boats or human interlopers other than ourselves. The colouring is as perfect, as varied and as utterly beyond description as that of Lake Louise. The lake is an Alpine gem, in whose bright surface are reflected the green of the forest that surrounds its shores, and the mountains that enclose it on either side, the huge bulk of Mount Schaffer and the curious pinnacles of the Wiwaxy Peaks. A couple of miles to the southwest, and reached by a good trail, is Lake McArthur, another mountain tarn only a little less charming than Lake O'Hara.

If one has only a limited time to spend in the Park, however, unquestionably it should be devoted to the Yoho Valley, on the north side of the railway. Several good roads and trails now lead to the valley from Field, by way of Emerald Lake, Burgess Pass and the Yoho River, so that the visitor has a choice of routes, and is assured of many enchanting views both going and coming.

The valley was explored as long ago as 1897 by Jean Habel, a famous German mountaineer, who spent seventeen days there and returned with such enthusiastic accounts of mountains, lakes and wonderful waterfalls that it was determined to make the valley accessible to tourists. A trail was commenced by the Canadian Pacific Railway in 1900, and since the organisation of the district into a national park this first attempt has been extended into a system of roads and trails giving access to every part of the valley. A delightful drive through "aisles of stately firs," and over a good wagon road, brings one to Emerald Lake, where the Railway Company, with its customary thoughtfulness, has provided a comfortable and picturesque chalet, situated on a wooded promontory. The lake, says Outram, is a "gem of perfect beauty, its colouring marvellously rich and vivid, and constantly changing under the shifting lights and shades." In its surface are mirrored the ramparts and precipices of Mount Wapta and Mount Burgess and the snowy glaciers of President Mountain.

From Emerald Lake, the road winds up the valley, with ever changing views of the mighty peaks on either side. We are waiting, however, for our first glimpse of the glory of the valley, Takakkaw Falls, remembering the meaning of the Indian name, "It is wonderful!" Presently we come out of the forest, the falls are before us across the valley, and we can do nothing but echo the exclamation of the Indians.

To borrow again from Sir James Outram, "the torrent issuing from an icy cavern rushes tempestuously down a deep, winding chasm till it gains the verge of the unbroken cliff, leaps forth in sudden wildness for a hundred and fifty feet, and then in a stupendous column of pure white sparkling water, broken by giant jets descending rocket-like and wreathed in volumed spray, dashes upon the rocks almost a thousand feet below, and breaking into a milky series of cascading rushes for five hundred feet more, swirls into the swift current of the Yoho River."

Mary M. Vaux, W. S. Vaux, and G. Vaux, Jr.

TWIN FALLS

(*Yoho Valley*)

Farther up the valley we come to the less imposing but even more picturesque Twin Falls, and the appropriately named Laughing Fall, where the Upper Yoho leaps down the mountain side. It is impossible to give more than a mere impression of the charms of this delightful valley. It would indeed be difficult to find anywhere else a more perfect grouping of the elements of Rocky Mountain scenery, great peaks and glaciers, stately forests and meadows carpeted with wildflowers, rushing streams, lakes of the most exquisite colouring, and a group of waterfalls as varied in character as they are all strikingly beautiful.

VII

AROUND THE ILLECILLEWAET

As we leave Field behind, and slide rapidly down the western slope of the Rockies to the Columbia valley, revelling in the ever-changing panorama of stately peaks, and enjoying it all from a comfortable arm-chair in the observation car, it is interesting to recall the very different journey of Sir Sandford Fleming in 1883. He had been the chief engineer of the Canadian Pacific Railway surveys from 1871 to 1880, and had strongly advocated the Yellowhead Pass route through the mountains in preference to the Kicking Horse Pass. His judgment has since been vindicated by the selection of the former route by both the new Canadian transcontinental roads, the Grand Trunk Pacific and the Canadian Northern.

When the Canadian Pacific Railway was taken over from the Dominion Government by a syndicate, it was decided to build through the Kicking Horse. In 1883 the rails had been laid as far as Calgary, at the eastern entrance to the mountains, actually before there was any certainty that it would be possible to get through by the southern route. The Kicking Horse Pass was believed to be feasible though presenting many serious engineering difficulties, but that only took them through the main range. There were still the Selkirks and the Gold Range to cross, before they could reach Kamloops on the North Thompson River, beyond which the route had been selected and the rails partly laid; but all the information the Company then had was a vague report that a route might be found over the former by Rogers Pass and over the latter by Eagle Pass. Very little was known of either.

The directors of the Company were between the horns of a dilemma. If they went ahead, they might find themselves stranded on the east side of the Selkirks. On the other hand, to abandon the route would mean the loss of millions of dollars already expended in bringing the rails to Calgary. In their difficulty they sent for Fleming, and asked him to go over the ground between Calgary and Kamloops and let them know if the railway could be taken through the three ranges, the Rockies, Selkirks and Gold Range. One can imagine the famous engineer chuckling over the situation. He had recommended the Yellowhead route; his advice had been rejected; and now the advocates of the rival Kicking Horse route were compelled to fall back upon him, to beg him of all men to demonstrate the practicability of the southern route. He accepted the commission, went over the route thoroughly, and was able to report that the railway could be taken through from Calgary to Kamloops. What he saw, however, was very far from shaking his former opinion that the Yellowhead Pass route was preferable in every way to that by the Kicking Horse.

This is merely introductory to a paragraph or two from Sir Sandford Fleming's account of his journey through the mountains in 1883—something to ponder over as we rush down the same wild valley in our luxurious observation car.

Fleming had left the railway at Calgary, and with ponies and pack-horses had slowly forced his way to the summit of the main range, and was now climbing down the valley of the Kicking Horse to the Columbia. We pick him up one morning, somewhere about the western boundary of what is now Yoho Park.

"The mist hangs like a thick curtain, concealing everything not directly near the camp-fire. But we start; the six pack-horses in front with their loads standing out from their backs, giving the creatures the appearance of so many dromedaries. Dave rides ahead with the bell-horse, then the pack-horses follow, and the horsemen bring up the rear to see that none stray behind. Our journey this day is over exceedingly rough ground. We have to cross gorges so narrow that a biscuit might be thrown from the last horse descending to the bell-horse six hundred feet ahead, ascending the opposite side.

Mary M. Vaux, W. S. Vaux, and G. Vaux, Jr.

MOUNT SIR DONALD AND ILLECILLEWAET GLACIER

"The fires have been running through the wood and are still burning; many of the half-burnt trees have been blown down by last night's gale, obstructing the trail and making advance extremely difficult.... Fortunately there is no wind. The air is still and quiet, otherwise we would run the risk of blackened trunks falling around us, possibly upon the animals or ourselves, even at the best seriously to have impeded our progress, if such a mischance did not make an advance impossible until the wind should moderate.

Canadian Pacific Railway Company

A BIT OF THE ILLECILLEWAET

"We move forward down and up gorges hundreds of feet deep, amongst rocky masses where the poor horses have to clamber as best they can amid sharp points and deep crevices, running the constant risk of a broken leg. The trail now takes another character. A series of precipices run sheer up from the boiling current to form a contracted canyon. A path has therefore been traced along the hill side, ascending to the elevation of some seven or eight hundred feet. For a long distance not a vestige of vegetation is to be seen. On the steep acclivity our line of advance is narrow, so narrow that there is scarcely a foothold; nevertheless we have to follow for some six miles this thread of trail, which seemed to us by no means in excess of the requirements of the chamois and the mountain goat.

"We cross clay, rock and gravel slides at a giddy height. To look down gives one an uncontrollable dizziness, to make the head swim and the view unsteady, even with men of tried nerves. I do not think that I can ever forget that terrible walk. We are from five to eight hundred feet high on a path of from ten to fifteen inches wide and at some points almost obliterated, with slopes above and below us so steep that a stone would roll into the torrent in the abyss below."

A few miles more, and Fleming emerged from the valley of the Kicking Horse and stood on the banks of the Columbia, with the mighty walls of the Rockies and Selkirks towering above him to the east and to the west. His way through the Selkirks was by the same route that we now follow on the railway, and it brought him in time to the summit of Rogers Pass, and the first sight of the since famous Illecillewaet Glacier. As we follow in his footsteps, we find ourselves entering the third great National Park of Canada—appropriately named Glacier Park, for from any one of its great peaks one may count a score of these wonderful ice rivers.

The Selkirk Range strikes even the unobservant traveller as markedly different from the main range of the Rockies. The colouring of the rocks is more varied and less sombre; the valleys are deeper and clothed with dense forests of gigantic evergreens, cedar, spruce, hemlock, Douglas fir, and up near the extreme limit of vegetation the beautiful Lyall's larch; and the snowfall is very much heavier than in the more easterly range. From its geographical position the Selkirk Range intercepts a large percentage of the moisture borne inland from the Pacific, which would otherwise reach the Rockies, and this with the deep valleys has resulted in a vegetation that is almost tropical in its luxuriance, and infinite in its variety, something over five hundred different flowers alone having been discovered in Glacier Park.

Geologists tell us that the Selkirks are very much older than the main range, that in fact they were hoary with antiquity when as the result of some vast convulsion of nature the Rockies were born. The brilliantly coloured quartzites of the Selkirks belong to an age so remote that the mere thought of it is enough to make one's head reel. In their day they looked out to the eastward upon a great sea, covering what are to-day vast fertile plains, and the sea washed over the place where the giants of the Rockies now lift their snowy heads proudly into the heavens.

Compared with Rocky Mountain Park, Glacier Park is a comparatively small reservation, covering an area of 468 square miles, but any one capable of appreciating the glories of mountain scenery, the great valleys with their picturesque torrents and waterfalls and riotous vegetation; the upper slopes with their bewildering array of alpine flowers, dryas, anemones and mountain lilies, red and white heather, glowing masses of painter's-brush, yellow and purple asters, blue gentians and yellow columbines, delicate moss campion and the dear little forget-me-not; the dizzy precipices and dazzling glaciers; and the conquered summits with their glorious outlook over a world of indescribable wildness and grandeur, — will find here a region of perpetual delight, where he may roam afield for weeks each day on an entirely new trail.

Although the park as a park did not exist until long after his visit, and good roads and trails now take the place of the rough paths he had to follow, William Spotswood Green's *Among the Selkirk Glaciers*, is still the most satisfactory and entertaining introduction that one can find, or wish for, to this mountain playground. Green came to the Selkirks in 1888, after years of delightful experience in the Alps and the great mountains of New Zealand. He left with the conviction that he had seen nothing elsewhere more impressive or more fascinating than these mountains of British Columbia. "Dark green forest, rushing streams, purple peaks, silvery ice, a cloudless sky, and a most transparent atmosphere," he says, "all combine to form a perfect Alpine paradise."

One of his first visits was to the Illecillewaet Glacier, which then entailed a slow and more or less painful scramble through a wilderness of fallen timber, tangled thickets of alder scrub, and the appropriately named devil's club. To-day one reaches the foot of the glacier by way of a delightful and well-kept trail through the forest, the trail starting from the doors of Glacier House, the large and comfortable hotel maintained by the Canadian Pacific Railway at the headquarters of the park.

On the way he had an opportunity of observing the tremendous destructive power of avalanches. "The hemlock, balsam, and Douglas firs, though as stout as ships' masts, had been snapped off close to their roots; some were torn up and driven long distances from where they grew, and lay in heaps, but the general position of the trunks pointed distinctly to the direction from which the destroying avalanche had come. Even the boulders of the moraine showed signs of having been shifted, some of them huge blocks of quartzite, one I measured 50 X 33 X 24 feet. No better illustration could be presented of the overwhelming power of an avalanche, though composed of nothing else than the accumulation of a winter's snow."

On this or another expedition, Green was introduced to the idiosyncrasies of the Indian pony or cayuse. One had been taken as a pack horse, and picked his way demurely along the trail for some time, with that air of meek innocence which always imposes upon the tenderfoot. Suddenly, without a moment's warning, and for no apparent reason, he was "seized with a paroxysm of buck-jumping; the packs flew off, he rolled down through the ferns and rocks, and then, perfectly satisfied with his performance, stood patiently while we restored our goods on his back." The incident will bring back many similar experiences to those who have camped in the Rocky Mountains. One is almost tempted to chuckle over Green's bewilderment. It is generally found that there is reason in the pony's madness. When he runs unexpectedly into a hornet's nest, the most natural thing in the world is to get away from it as quickly as possible, and as a rule the quickest way is to roll down hill.

Exasperating as the cayuse can be on many occasions, no one who has any sense of humour or any appreciation of animal intelligence can fail in time to grow very fond of a horse that has been his companion on many wild mountain trails, that has carried him safely through raging torrents, and sometimes shared his meal beside the camp fire. A good pony will follow unerringly a trail that is indistinguishable to even an experienced guide; he will carry an able-bodied man, or a much heavier pack, all day over a trail that would kill an eastern horse; he will pick his way through a tangle of fallen timber with an instinct that is almost uncanny; and he will do all this on the uncertain feed of mountain camps. He is a true philosopher, a creature of shrewd common sense, pluck, endurance, and rare humour, a good fellow, and a rare friend.

Green made the first attempt to scale Mount Sir Donald, the splendid peak that almost overshadows Glacier House. He selected what proved to be an impracticable route, and was forced to return without reaching the summit. The mountain has since been repeatedly climbed, and is now with Mount Stephen in the Rockies the most popular peak for mountain-climbers in the Canadian parks. Thanks to the Swiss guides who are stationed here throughout the season, any one of reasonable endurance and with a head for dizzy heights or depths, can now make his way to the summit of Sir Donald, 10,808 feet above the sea, and be rewarded with a view that will more than compensate him for the fatigue.

Although mountain-climbing in the Canadian Rockies has been singularly free from accidents, there have of course occasionally been narrow escapes, and one of these is graphically described in *Among the Selkirk Glaciers*. Green and a companion had climbed to the summit of Mount Bonney, a great peak some miles west of Sir Donald, and were returning, when they made the usual mistake of trying a short cut to avoid a tedious piece of climbing. There seemed to be a way down a very steep snow slope, and Green went ahead on the rope to test it, while his companion anchored himself as firmly as possible in the snow above. They were of course "roped" in the usual mountaineering fashion.

"I turned my face to the slope," says Green, "and holding on to the rope kicked my toes in and went over the brink. I took the precaution, too, of burying my axe up to its head at every step. Just below the brink there was a projecting crag. This I thought would give a firm footing before testing the snow slope. I got one foot on to it and was taking it as gently as possible when the rock gave way, a large piece of snow went with it and fell on the slope twenty feet below.

"I stuck my knees into the snow, but felt my whole weight was on the rope. Then I heard a swishing noise in the air, and glancing downwards saw that the whole snow slope had cracked across and was starting away down towards the valley in one huge avalanche. H. hauled cautiously but firmly on the rope, and getting what grip I could with toes, knees and ice-axe I was quickly in a safe position, and the two of us standing side by side watched the clouds of snow filling the abyss below and the huge masses bounding outwards. We listened to the sullen roar which gradually subsided and all again was quiet."

A. Knechtel

THE HIGH FRONTIER OF BRITISH COLUMBIA

A. O. Wheeler

ON THE SUMMIT OF SIR DONALD

It was probably this same stout rope by which Green pulled himself back to safety, of which he elsewhere gives the history, quite an eventful one, though sadly ignoble in its latter days. "Its first good work was to save the lives of some of our party in a bad slip, near the summit of the Balmhorn on the Bernese Overland. It was next used as the mizzen topping-lift of a fifteen-ton yawl. It was my tent-rope in the New Zealand Alps. It was the bridle used on a deep-sea trawl that went down to 1000 fathoms beneath the surface of the Atlantic. It trained a colt. Now it was in our diamond hitch; and I regret to say that its old age was disgraced by its being used for cording one of my boxes on the voyage home."

Compared with Rocky Mountains Park and Yoho Park, Glacier Park at present is somewhat deficient in roads and trails, those that have been opened all radiating from headquarters and extending not more than six or eight miles in any direction. This, however, will be remedied in a few years, the park being still very young, and in the meantime it is not an unmixed evil to those who care to get off the beaten track. Old Indian trails follow all the rivers and creeks throughout the park, and though these will be more or less obliterated and blocked with fallen timber, a competent guide can always be relied upon to take you to any corner of the park, and when you have found a good camping ground, with feed for the horses, a sparkling stream at your feet, and a circle of noble peaks smiling down upon you, you will, if you are the right sort, thank your stars that railways and hotels and roads lie far away in another world beyond the mountains. To really enjoy this sensation of out-of-the-worldness, however, you must have brought with you a sufficient supply of worldly eatables.

Of the available trails, one leads up to Rogers Pass, at the summit of the Selkirks, with Mount Macdonald on one side and Mount Tupper on the other. These two great peaks were named after the famous Canadian statesmen, Sir John Macdonald and Sir Charles Tupper. The latter, after watching the growth of Canada from a group of weak and scattered colonies to a strong and ambitious Dominion, is still alive in England in his ninety-third year.

In the opposite direction, good trails lead to the Illecillewaet Glacier, and to Asulkan Pass and the Asulkan Glacier, from which it is possible to reach a group of magnificent peaks, Castor and Pollux, The Dome, Clarke, Swanzy, and a little farther to the west Bonney and Smart. On the opposite side lies the vast Illecillewaet snow-field.

From Glacier House, again, a good carriage road takes you west parallel with the railway and the Illecillewaet River, towards Cougar Mountain and Ross Peak. Eventually this will be extended to the Nakimu Caves. At present a trail follows the same route to the Caves, and around Mount Cheops to Rogers Pass, thus providing a round trip, from Glacier House to the Caves, thence to Rogers Pass, and back to Glacier House again.

The Nakimu Caves were discovered accidentally some nine years ago, and are said to be well worth visiting. They are in charge of C. H. Deutschmann, who discovered and explored them, and thanks to his competent guidance and the facilities that have been provided it is now possible for any one to visit and examine this curious freak of nature. It will be more convenient to describe the Caves in another chapter.

Those who would really wish to know the character, extent and variety of the scenery in Glacier Park and the great mountain range of which it is only a small part, are recommended to consult A. O. Wheeler's delightful guide-book, *The Selkirk Mountains*, and the same author's exhaustive work published by the Dominion Government, *The Selkirk Range*. These are not only readable and author-itative, but with the exception of Green's *Among the Selkirk Glaciers*, they are the only books available on this very important region.[3]

---

[3] Since the above was written Howard Palmer's *Mountaineering and Exploration in the Selkirks* has been published, making a very important addition to the scanty literature on the subject.

VIII

THE CAVES OF NAKIMU

T HE traveller who for the sake of contrast or variety desires to enjoy a sensation as different as possible from the glorious panorama of mountain and valley, lake and waterfall, rich in colouring, instinct with the life-giving qualities of sun and air, cannot do better than spend an afternoon in the Caves of Nakimu. It will be to him as though he were transported from the domains of the Upper Gods to the gloomy realm of Pluto. Under the guardianship of C. H. Deutschmann, the official guide, whose cabin stands across a small ravine from the visitor's camp, the caves may be explored with safety and a reasonable degree of comfort. The facilities for getting about the caves and underground passages is still rather primitive, but sufficient to ensure the safety of visitors, and you have the advantage of seeing everything in its natural state. One can appreciate the hardihood of Deutschmann, who alone, and with nothing but tallow candles, explored caves and potholes and corridors. As Mr. Wheeler has said, "Added to the thick darkness, there was always the fierce, vibrating roar of subterranean torrents, a sound most nerve-shaking in a position sufficiently uncanny without it. Huge cracks had to be crossed and precipitous descents made in pitch darkness, where a misstep meant death or disablement."

The caves extend into the south slopes of Mount Ursus Major and Mount Cheops and into the north slopes of Cougar Mountain. The rock out of which the caves have been carved, by Nature's patient craftsmen, is described as a "marbleized limestone, varying in colour from very dark blue, almost black, shot with ribbons of calcite, through varying shades of grey to almost white." There are no stalactites or stalagmites worth mentioning.

The caves are in three sections, known as the Gopher Bridge, Mill Bridge, and the Gorge. The following description is taken from Arthur O. Wheeler's account of his survey in 1905.

Canadian Pacific Railway Company

THE WEIRD CAVES OF NAKIMU

The Gopher Bridge caves are approached by two openings, one known as the

Old Entrance, the other as the New Entrance. Mr. Wheeler used the former in his visit, and took his observation by the light of gas lamps and magnesium wire. Not far from the entrance he came to a place where the passage dropped suddenly into space. "Standing on a ledge that overhangs a black abyss," he says, "the eye is first drawn by a subterranean waterfall heard roaring immediately on the left. It appears to pour from a dark opening above it. Below, between black walls of rock, may be seen the foam-flecked torrent hurtling down the incline until lost in dense shadows. Overhead, fantastic spurs and shapes reach out into the blackness, and the entire surroundings are so weird and uncanny that it is easy to imagine Dante seated upon one of these spurs deriving impressions for his Inferno. As the brilliant light gives out, the thick darkness makes itself felt, and instinctively you feel to see if Charon is not standing beside you. This subterranean stream with its unearthly surroundings is suggestive of the Styx and incidentally supplied the name Avernus for the cavern of the waterfall." The Cavern of Avernus is reached by the New Entrance, through a small passage.

Cougar Brook emerges from the Gopher Bridge caves 450 feet down the valley, and after pouring down a rock-cut known as the Flume, disappears into the Mill Bridge caves. The entrance is some thirty feet to the east, through a cleft in the rock. A passageway of 400 feet leads to an irregularly shaped chamber known as the Auditorium, through which Cougar Brook roars its way. "Faint daylight enters through the passageway of the waters, making the place look dim and mysterious." The passageway is broken at intervals by potholes, ten or fifteen feet deep, necessitating a series of rough ladders, and in one case a floating bridge as the pothole is half filled with water.

Emerging from the Mill Bridge caves, the brook runs for 300 feet through a deep gorge spanned by two natural bridges, and then enters the third series of caves. Creeping down a long passageway, with the dull roar of the stream ever in your ears, you come to a sharp descent of twelve feet with natural footholds, but persons unaccustomed to climbing are advised to use a rope to steady the descent. "Here the brook is heard far down rushing through some rock-cut with a dull intermittent pounding like the blows of a giant sledge-hammer."

A passage to the right brings you to the Dropping Cave, with walls and ceiling of dark blue limestone streaked with white calcite, and water dropping everywhere from the roof. From the eastern end of this cave a narrow passage leads to the Witch's Ball Room, a triangular cavern whose floor is broken by deep cracks "leading down to where the underground stream roars threateningly." Beyond this are several other passages and smaller chambers, the farthest known as the Pit.

Another entrance to the Gorge caves, known as Entrance No. 3, leads first to a small cavern, reached by a ladder from above. A very narrow passage, which must be negotiated by means of a rope, brings you to a ledge overlooking a sheer drop of sixty feet.

From one of the passages leading to the Pit, a cavern is reached, named the Turbine, owing to the noise from waterspouts resembling the sound of water falling into the pit of a turbine. Farther on is the Art Gallery, so called from the "florescent designs of overlying carbonate of lime, in colour from cream to delicate salmon."

Beyond the Art Gallery, a long passage brings you to a narrow twisted opening named the Gimlet, and to two ancient potholes leading to unknown depths, and "profusely ornamented with florescent incrustation." One of these is named the Dome, from its perfect form. A passage from the other leads to the Judgment Hall.

In this section of the Gorge Caves the subterranean river crosses the main passage some depth below, and its roar is now heard from the right side. A narrow opening leads to the Carbonate Grotto which has some fine floral designs. Another passage of 130 feet brings you to a crack in the wall, from which a descent of 57 feet leads to the Judgment Hall mentioned before. This is the largest of the caves, 200 feet wide and from 40 to 50 feet high.

From the Judgment Hall, other passages lead to the White Grotto, so named from the beauty and delicacy of its ornamentations; and the Bridal Chamber, also covered with floral designs.

The Caves of Nakimu are of peculiar interest to the geologist, as the limestone of which they are composed is rare in the Selkirks. The subterranean stream which forms the principal feature of the caves is also a rare phenomenon either in the Rockies or Selkirks. There is some difference of opinion as to the origin of the caves. The passageways are unquestionably due in a measure to water-erosion, but Mr. Wheeler, who has given the matter much study, is convinced that a more potent agency has been at work. "It is not unreasonable to assume," he says, "that a seismic disturbance once shattered this bed of crystalline limestone and precipitated Cougar Creek into subterranean channels which the water and time have enlarged to their present size; moreover, that subsequent shocks are responsible for the large quantities of débris that litter their floors. This hypothesis would explain the crack of the Gorge and similar chasms beneath the surface."

IX

MOUNTAIN CLIMBING AND CLIMBERS

SOME of the most notable exploits in mountain-climbing in the Canadian Rockies have been by officers of the Dominion Government, such as J. J. McArthur and A. O. Wheeler, merely as incidents to their serious work of topographical surveying. The advent of the mountaineer as such, and the development of the region as a mountaineer's paradise, dates from the visit of William Spotswood Green in 1888. Probably his book, which appeared two years later, did as much as anything else to bring others to the Canadian mountains. At any rate, in 1890, members of the English and Swiss Alpine Clubs, and the Appalachian Mountain Club of Boston, visited the Selkirks, and returned with enthusiastic accounts of the new field available to mountain climbers.

The visit of Professor Charles E. Fay, of the Appalachian Club, led to the formation of an Alpine section of that club, and later to the organisation of the American Alpine Club. The Alpine Club of Canada came into being in 1906, and since that date, under the notable leadership of A. O. Wheeler, has rapidly gained strength and influence, drawing into its fold an ever-increasing number of those who find keen pleasure and a widening and strengthening of all their faculties in the splendid sport of mountain-climbing, or in the mere dwelling from day to day in the companionship of some of the most noble works of Nature.

The earlier explorations of mountain-climbers, following that of Green, were confined pretty well to the Selkirks, but as interest spread the great peaks of the main range were attempted, and one after another succumbed to the attacks of such notable climbers as Outram, Fay and Parker; Collie, Stutfield and Woolley; Abbott, Eggers, Weed and Thompson, and the prince of all mountain-climbers, Whymper. A brief account will now be given of some of these ascents in the Rockies, leaving the Selkirks to another chapter.

Byron Harmon

THE ASSAULT

Byron Harmon

VICTORY AT LAST

Dr. Fay made an attempt upon Mount Goodsir in 1901, with Outram and Scattergood, and the veteran Swiss guide Christian Häsler, but owing to the exceptionally dangerous condition of the snow near the summit the party were forced to turn back at the foot of the final peak. Two years later this superb peak of the Ottertail Range was again attacked by Dr. Fay, accompanied this time by Professor Parker, and the guides Christian Kaufmann and Häsler. Dr. Fay has described both climbs in the *Canadian Alpine Journal*, 1907, from which the following account is taken.

The party camped at the foot of the mountain, in 1901, and set out at daybreak the following morning. A stiff climb brought them to the base of a steep cliff beyond which rose the final peak. "Before us," says Dr. Fay, "rose this beetling face of dark rock, with little snow patches here and there revealing possible stations, between which only cracks and slight protuberances offered scanty holds for foot and hand." With great care, however, they finally reached the top of the cliff. Here, however, they were brought to a standstill.

"A most ominous situation revealed itself. The final peak was before us, and its summit hardly three hundred feet distant—a great white hissing mass,—a precipice on the hidden left side, a steep snow-slope of perhaps 65 to 70 degrees on the right. Under the July sun its whole surface was seemingly in a state of flux, slipping over the underlying mass with a constant, threatening hiss. A second narrow arête led across to this final summit. This, too, was corniced, and in a remarkable way. The swirl of the wind had produced an unusual spectacle. At the beginning and at the end, the cornice hung out to the right; in the middle, a reversed section of it overhung the abyss on the left.

"The two similar ones could doubtless have been passed. To cross the middle section meant trusting ourselves to the sun-beaten slope already in avalanching condition. Indeed, while we studied it, and as if to furnish the final argument to our debate, the snow on our right impinging against the cornice broke away, and down went a well-developed avalanche a couple of thousand feet over that much-tilted surface, and vanished in a sheer plunge that landed it perhaps three thousand feet below that. It was a suggestive and persuasive sight. Feeling sure that we had seen enough for one day we beat a careful retreat."

The 1903 climb was practically identical with that of 1901, but the conditions were entirely different. "The broken arête was indeed under a draping of recent snow, but no cornice was in evidence. It was 'plain sailing'—and yet very interesting, for the arête was so narrow and thin that one astride it could have his left leg vertical over a sheer drop, at first indeed overhanging, of hundreds if not thousands of feet, while its mate pointed down that 76° slope of snow, as silent now as it was noisy in 1901. At eleven o'clock we were on the summit—Goodsir was ours. The repulse of two years ago was forgotten, and our affections went out to the graceful peak, no longer a sullen monster, and, for the joys of that one glorious hour spent on its pure snowy summit, we granted it our love for a lifetime."

The same year Professor Parker, with the guides Christian and Hans Kaufmann, made a successful attack on Mount Hungabee, the grim "Chieftain" (as the Indian name is translated) that stands guard at the head of Paradise Valley.

The party left the Chalet at Lake Louise on the morning of July 20th, and travelling up the Valley of the Ten Peaks, crossed over by a high pass into Prospectors Valley where they camped. The following morning at 3.50 they left camp and tramped up the valley to the foot of Hungabee. A steep slope brought them to the foot of a vertical cliff, the only practical means of ascent being by way of a narrow chimney filled with ice. Christian Kaufmann went ahead, leaving his companions at the foot of the cliff until he should reach the top.

"It was only," says Professor Parker, "by watching the rope that Hans and I could judge the progress Christian was making above us. For minutes at a time, it seemed, the rope would be motionless, then inch by inch it would slowly disappear up the chimney, and the crash of falling rocks and ice would warn us that we must cling even more closely and find what protection we could beneath the rocky wall." At last Christian gave the signal to follow, and the others soon stood beside him at the top of the chimney. Above them a smooth, steep slope led to the final peak, over which they made their way without difficulty. The summit was now only a few hundred feet above, but the arête or ridge leading to it was broken by vertical cliffs and quite unscalable. The only alternative was to traverse a tremendously steep snow-slope at the base of the cliffs and so reach the final cone.

"We did not," says Professor Parker, "discuss the possible dangers of such a course, but cautiously made our way beneath the cliffs, turned a most sensational corner almost in mid-air above Paradise Valley, and then scaled a nearly perpendicular cliff by means of a convenient crack. We were now on the arête but a very short distance from the summit. Only one more difficulty confronted us: a narrow 'gabel,' or break in the arête, only a few feet in width it is true, but with a nearly sheer descent of thousands of feet on either side. This gabel must be crossed to reach the summit. The arête was far too narrow to allow a jump being made with safety; so, slowly and carefully, while firmly grasping the rock on one side, Christian thrust his feet forward until they touched the other and his body bridged the chasm; then a strong forward swing, and he stood safely beyond the gap. For me, aided by the rope, the matter was far less difficult, and soon we made our way over the intervening arête, gained the corniced summit, and Hungabee, the grim old 'Chieftain,' at last was conquered."

Among many daring climbs in the Canadian Rockies, few have been more sensational than the successful ascent of Pinnacle Mountain, on the eastern side of Paradise Valley, by J. W. A. Hickson in 1909. The following is borrowed from Mr. Hickson's spirited account of the climb in the *Canadian Alpine Journal*, 1910. Several determined efforts had been made to capture the peak during the summer of 1907, but the season was unfavourable for mountaineering, and in every case the climbers were driven back. The critical point was at the foot of an almost vertical tower, a few hundred feet below the summit, but only two possible means of surmounting this final wall presented themselves. One was by way of a chimney or crack in the wall, and the other in traversing the face of the mountain along an extremely narrow ledge of peculiarly rotten rock. The first had been tried unsuccessfully in 1907. The latter formed the route of the 1909 expedition. Mr. Hickson was accompanied by two Swiss guides, Edouard Fuez, Jr., and Rudolf Aemmer.

Grand Trunk Pacific Railway Company

THE MONARCH OF THE ROCKIES

(From a painting by George Horne Russell)

"It was realised," says Mr. Hickson, "that only very slow progress could be made in this direction, for the disintegrated tawny-coloured limestone rock was of a most treacherous character. It was covered for the most part with a glaze of ice, which when disturbed had a tendency to bring the eroded limestone away with it. It was hard to say whether the rock sustained the ice or vice versa; perhaps the support, such as it was, was mutual.

"In our attempt to turn a sharp angle I found myself sitting for about ten minutes—but for what seemed more like half an hour—astride a rocky protuberance, which appeared likely to give way at any moment, while Fuez was endeavouring to find a good footing on the other side. For a few minutes I almost regretted that I had come; for there was a sheer drop on either side of probably 2,000 feet. At many places there were no handholds; and we dared not touch the rocks with our ice-axes lest we should precipitate downwards the insecure supports we were standing on. We were very much in the position of flies on a nearly vertical wall covered with sand which from time to time was crumbling off. There was no defined ledge to follow.

"Advancing gingerly with cat-like tread, and avoiding any spring or jerk which might detach the insecure footholds and leave us hanging precariously, Fuez picked out places here and there which offered the chance of a support, and we were glad when we found a piece of rock an inch or two wide and a few inches long on a part of which a nailed boot-edge could obtain a transitory grip. It is remarkable how very small a projection, if not slippery, will suffice for a temporary hold. Fortunately not one of the party once slipped; thus avoiding any test as to how far he could have been held by the others. Luckily, also, we had lots of rope, so that we could allow about twenty-five feet between each person, and thus enabled us at times to manœuvre into better positions.

"Our nerves throughout this period of two hours, during most of which only one of us moved at a time, were at considerable tension; not a moment of slackness or diminution of watchfulness being allowable. A keen lookout was constantly demanded to meet an emergency which was not at all improbable. Nothing could be taken or was taken for granted, except that everything was unreliable and an accident might be expected. This is perhaps why none occurred.

"After advancing persistently and almost horizontally along the face of the wall for two hours, we saw an unexpected chance of reaching our goal more speedily than we had latterly hoped. This was offered by a large couloir leading to the 'saddle' between the black tower and the summit of the mountain, which is not much higher than the top of the tower. Fairly steep and broad, the gulch contained some ice and snow.

"As we got down into it Fuez turned to me and said, 'I think we've got him,' of which I was already convinced. Crossing the couloir we rapidly ascended the rocks on the left side and at its top, to our great surprise, landed on a bed of shale, which by an easy slope led in a few minutes to the summit."

After resting for a time on the summit, and enjoying the wonderful panorama of peaks and valleys, they prepared to make the descent. It being more trying and precarious to climb down than up a mountain, the guides were unwilling to follow the rather hazardous route they had taken on the way to the summit, if it could be avoided, and it was therefore decided to attempt the chimney, on the other side of the mountain.

"We followed a narrow but firm ledge for about fifteen minutes from the saddle around the southerly tower. It then became necessary to reconnoitre to see if the route proposed were further feasible. So the second guide Aemmer, assisted by Fuez, went ahead and soon returned to say that we could get down by roping off. This led to one of the most interesting and exciting bits of the whole climb.

"At the corner or angle where the ledge terminated there was a peculiar arrangement of rock which had resulted in the formation of a small square hole with nothing but sky to be seen on the further side. Under this hole there was a gap in the ledge of about three feet, with a drop of about fifteen feet into a dark pit beneath. To cross the gap it was necessary to lie down flat upon the ledge on the one side with face to the rock, stretch your feet to the rock on the other, your body thus spanning the gap, then draw yourself through the hole and gradually swing yourself into an upright position by the help of the rope and the handholds in the further wall of rock. It looked a more trying operation than it actually was because one had to turn somewhat sharply on emerging from the hole in order to stand on a somewhat slender ledge. But there is practically no danger; when one is firmly held on the rope by guides, whose caution and resourcefulness, here as elsewhere, were admirable, and have fully justified the confidence which I have always reposed in their ability.

"Having, with mutual assistance, all three surmounted this difficulty and having advanced a little further down the side of the tower, we perceived a way into the chimney already referred to, about sixty feet above its base. Here it was obvious that the only way of getting down was to rope off. Amongst other paraphernalia we had brought with us an extra short piece of rope which would serve as a loop. It was now slung around a firm piece of rock, which was rendered more adaptable to the purpose by a little hammering, while through the loop was passed a second rope about 120 feet long. This being doubled still gave us the required length.

"I went down first, being held besides on another rope, so that no serious mishap could have overtaken me. For the first forty feet there were practically no footholds to be found, a fact for which we were prepared; but fortunately the rock was good—indeed, this is the only bit of firm rock on the mountain—and I got safely down and out of the chimney, after swinging once or twice like a bundle of goods, without any worse experience than having my clothing a little torn and with the feeling that there might be a permanent groove around the centre of my body.

"Fuez descended next and took a photograph of Aemmer sitting at the top. As Aemmer was descending he disturbed a small stone which danced down with great force and, to Fuez's chagrin, cut off about twenty feet from the lower end of his fine manilla rope. We then pulled down the rope, but of course, had to leave behind the loop, which may be serviceable to some other party."

One is tempted to repeat the story of the first successful ascent of Mount Deltaform, described by Wilcox as the "most difficult mountain yet ascended in the Canadian Rockies;" and of Wilcox's own climb up Mount Temple, but both are readily accessible in the *Rockies of Canada*. Some idea of the magnitude of the task of scaling Deltaform may be got from the fact that an unusually strong climbing party consisting of Professor H. C. Parker, Dr. A. Eggers, and the Swiss guides Hans and Christian Kaufmann, were nearly twenty-two hours in conquering the peak, "after a reconnaissance and repulse two days before."

This sketch of mountain-climbing in the main range of the Canadian Rockies, designed merely to give as far as possible in the words of the actors, some idea of the experiences incident to this king of sports, may close with an account of the first ascent of Crows Nest Mountain, one of the most difficult climbs in the Southern Canadian Rockies. P. D. McTavish tells the story in the *Canadian Alpine Journal*, 1907.

Byron Harmon

SNOW MUSHROOMS

In August, 1905, Mr. McTavish, with three friends, reached the base of the mountain and after several attempts which ended in quite impossible precipices, found a great crevice leading up about 400 feet and "resembling the space left in a whole cheese when a thin wedge-shaped piece has been removed." After resting for a time, they climbed up to a dome of rock which had obstructed their view. "With some difficulty we surmounted this, and found ourselves at the base of a beautifully straight, but very perpendicular, chimney, about six feet in width and two hundred feet high. This offered possibilities, so we immediately proceeded to climb to the top. Arriving there, a short shaly slope led to a similar chimney, up which we climbed. We now found ourselves at the top of the first circular band which begirts the mountain, and felt that victory was within our grasp.

George Kinney

ICICLES ON MOUNT ROBSON

(50 feet long)

"For some time we encountered a series of steep, rocky slopes and perpendicular faces, which led to a long slope of about one thousand feet, after which the climbing again became fairly difficult, but for only a short time, as we had reached the final dome, and at 12.15 o'clock we stood upon the summit." The entire climb had occupied about four hours.

X

CLIMBING IN THE SELKIRKS

ALTHOUGH W. S. Green had made an attempt in 1888, it was not until two years later that the giant of the Selkirks, Mount Sir Donald, was conquered. In July, 1890, Carl Sulzer and Emil Huber, of the Swiss Alpine Club, set out one morning about 4 o'clock from their camp at timber line, determined to find a way to the summit of the magnificent peak that shot up into the sky from their very feet. They had already studied the mountain from several points, and had selected a route that looked promising.

Crossing a small glacier, they turned up a couloir or gully terminating in a cave, above which the cliffs rose almost perpendicularly. The last part of the couloir became so narrow that the climbers had to force their way up by propping their bodies in the angle against the rocks on either side.

After a short rest, they started climbing up to the rocks of the southern ridge. It was stiff work in places even for such experienced mountaineers, but finally they reached the main crest and "gazed beyond the undulating tops of the foothills, upon the far-stretched row of blue peaks of the Rocky Mountains." Following the arête, or steep ridge of the mountain, and overcoming more than one difficulty as they went, they finally stood upon the summit, 10,800 feet above the sea.

From this isolated point they had a wonderful view of the Selkirks, with the main range of the Rockies in the distance. "The finest view presented itself in the southwest and south. Above the undulations of the Asulkan and Illecillewaet glaciers and opposite a deep valley, the fine group of Mount Dawson arose with its two corner-pillars, Mount Donkin and Mount Fox. But the most beautiful mountain of all appeared above the opening between Mount Dawson and Mount Donkin. It was Mount Purity, very properly so called, a snow mountain of the finest order."

Building a cairn to commemorate the first ascent of Sir Donald, and burying in it a bottle containing a record of the climb, ending with the jubilant words, "Three cheers for Switzerland," they retraced their way down the mountain, and were enthusiastically received at Glacier House, news of the first big climb in the Selkirks being immediately telegraphed east and west.

Toward the end of the same month, Herr Huber, accompanied by Messrs. Topham and Forster, of the English Alpine Club, made the first ascent of Mount

Purity, which had been named by Topham. They camped on the western slopes of the mountain, and set out for the summit about sunrise the following morning. The climb was a comparatively easy one to such seasoned mountaineers, and two hours' work brought the party to the summit.

Meanwhile Herr Sulzer was attacking another virgin peak, which he had named Swiss Peak. He had but one companion, with little or no experience in mountain-climbing, so that the attempt was a somewhat daring one.

Clambering up a series of grassy slopes and rock ridges, and crossing a glacier, they encountered steep rocks which afforded interesting though cautious climbing. A steep ice-slope now blocked further progress, and had to be negotiated by cutting "deep steps into the blue ice, which was as hard as glass." An hour's hard work brought them to the rocks on the opposite side. A comparatively easy climb along the ridge finally conducted them to the summit.

P. L. Tait

CLIMBING MOUNT RESPLENDANT

"The day," says Sulzer, "was perfectly clear. As far as the eye could see were innumerable mountain peaks all around. In the southern foreground the ice-girdled, central mass of the Selkirks, with its northern marking stone, the bold, fascinating Sir Donald, appeared especially beautiful. In the east, beyond the lower Selkirk peaks, the long row of haughty Rockies lay spread in partly rounded, partly broken shapes — a scene which I shall never forget. Sharply outlined, dark rock masses interchanged with lofty snow-tops; all showed clearly and glistened in the furthest distance, where, only fading, their faint outlines were lost in the horizon. The northern groups showed some particularly high peaks, and immense snow and ice-fields. Stately mountain chains in the west completed the scope." Herr Sulzer supposed the high peaks in the north to be Mount Brown and Mount Hooker, the famous peaks near the headwaters of the Athabaska which David Douglas the botanist estimated in 1827 to be between 16,000 and 17,000 feet in height, and which Professor A. P. Coleman of Toronto visited in 1893 and found to be about 9000 feet! In 1890, of course, they were still supposed to be the highest peaks in the Canadian Rockies, and many an ambitious mountain-climber hoped some day to stand upon their remote summits.

P. L. Tait

SUMMIT OF MOUNT RESPLENDANT

11,173 feet above the sea

As the reputed eminence of these now rather despised mountains was universally received for well-nigh three-quarters of a century, and is still recorded in a number of very respectable books of reference, it may not be without interest to quote Douglas's own account, as found in his Journal:

"Being well rested by one o'clock," (he was then at the summit of Athabaska Pass), "I set out with the view of ascending what seemed to be the highest peak on the north. Its height does not appear to be less than sixteen thousand or seventeen thousand feet above the level of the sea. After passing over the lower ridge I came to about 1200 feet of by far the most difficult and fatiguing walking I have ever experienced, and the utmost care was required to tread safely over the crust of snow.

"The view from the summit is of too awful a cast to afford pleasure. Nothing can be seen in every direction as far as the eye can reach except mountains towering above each other, rugged beyond description.... This peak, the highest yet known in the northern continent of America, I feel a sincere pleasure in naming 'Mount Brown,' in honour of R. Brown, Esq., the illustrious botanist.... A little to the southward is one nearly the same height, rising into a sharper point; this I named Mount Hooker, in honour of my early patron, the Professor of Botany in the University of Glasgow. This mountain, however, I was unable to climb."

Dr. J. Norman Collie, in commenting on this passage, says: "If Douglas climbed a seventeen-thousand-feet peak alone on a May afternoon, when the snow must have been pretty deep on the ground, all one can say is that he must have been an uncommonly active person. What, of course, he really did was to ascend the Mount Brown of Professor Coleman, which is about nine thousand feet high. These two fabulous Titans, therefore, which for nearly seventy years have been masquerading as the monarchs of the Canadian Rockies, must now be finally deposed."

In a letter from Mr. A. L. Mumm, of the English Alpine Club, who did some climbing in the Canadian Rockies in the autumn of 1913, he mentions that he climbed Mount Brown, and his aneroid made the height 8950 feet. Lest the humiliated mole-hill should fade away altogether, he is willing to admit that the accepted elevation of 9050 feet is probably correct. As for Mount Hooker, no one seems to have thought it worth while to climb it. In fact there is no great certainty as to which of the mountains about Athabaska Pass was Douglas' Mount Hooker. All that remains certain is that no peak in the neighbourhood remotely approaches the height given by the well-meaning botanist.

We may return to Herr Sulzer for a moment to note a curious incident that he mentions in connection with an expedition to a point west of Mount Tupper. "Seated on the highest elevation," he says, "I began to sketch a portion of the view, while black thunderclouds sailed towards the ridge from the valley. Suddenly, two stone slabs next to me and standing opposite each other begin to make a humming noise, the metal holder of my sketching pencil buzzes and my pick begins to crackle strongly, especially when I grasp it. Simultaneously, a slight rain sets in and my fingers, also moistened by the rain, buzz. My companion is taken by a sudden fright and is incapable of uttering a sound. The cause of this phenomenon was clear to me at once, although I was not fully aware of the degree of danger which it might include. We were in an electric cloud. I remembered to have heard a few thunder reports a short time before, issuing from the same cloud which had now reached us. The main volume of electricity stored up in it had escaped by lightning. The rest escaped when it reached the ridge, and to some extent, we ourselves involuntarily acted as conductors to the earth. A direct danger, therefore, was not present; for if the electric tension had still been great enough to generate lightning flashes, such would have been ejected before the clouds themselves touched the ridge. Nevertheless, the phenomenon was so strong that when I touched the pick on its metal mount, I felt a strong shock, and at night the play of sparks would undoubtedly have been visible."

The Minute Book at Glacier House contains an account of the first ascent of Mount Tupper, by Wolfgang Koehler, of Leipzig, in 1906. A translation of the narrative appeared in the *Canadian Alpine Journal*, 1909, from which the following is taken:

Koehler made the expedition with two Swiss guides, Edouard Fuez, Jr., and Gottfried Fuez. They walked from Glacier to Rogers Pass, and climbed up the trail to a hut provided for mountain-climbers, where they spent the night.

"The night was wonderfully beautiful, a cloudless sky and brilliant moonlight. Moreover, to be surrounded by the dear, beautiful mountains! How one's heart goes out to them! Towards 4 A. M. we got up, breakfasted, and started off at 5 A. M. We took the direction at first immediately behind the hut, then turned off to the right, and across the little icy creek, looking up to Rogers, Swiss and Fleming Peaks, Mount Tupper, Sifton and Grizzly. It was always up and then down again. We had innumerable gullies and streams to cross, until we reached the ridge at the end of two hours. We rested, and then started again, always following the ridge over icy blocks."

So they made their way, with more or less difficulty, until they reached a point where more serious problems confronted them. There were several possible routes, all involving pretty stiff climbing. One was finally selected as the most promising.

"In the middle of the right wall was a broad chimney, if only we could get up there direct. Two ridges appeared running parallel, which seemed to make the ascent possible. We climbed to the first ridge, next to the chimney, then up the first ridge in the chimney itself. So far we were still right. With the help of three picks and four hands Edouard got up a little higher, but quickly came down again. That could not be the right way. He tried then to go direct by the chimney, but that was not practicable, and so he had to come back.

"In between was Gottfried, who had successfully climbed up and stood in the chimney. I followed, Gottfried continued on, but a shower of big and small stones came down. It seemed as if everything was rotten, and, in spite of great care, not one of us could avoid bringing down the stones. We now went on the outside, round the rock, and came to a big flat, climbed a little broken chimney, and then got over a large rock. Soon we stood again before the wall. One piece appeared somewhat loose, and formed a breach, which gave us sufficient hold to get on to a small platform. From there it was a short, somewhat overhanging climb to the higher platform. 'This is the sort of place for people with long legs,' Edouard called out (I am 6 ft. 4 in.). 'Alas, we little ones have no chance.'

R. C. W. Lett

CLIMBING AMONG THE SERACS

"We now came back again to the ridge, came to a little *gendarme* (isolated rock tower or pinnacle) with a beautiful outlook down the valley, and climbed on, until we suddenly came to a wide platform. We had all three expected that the last piece to the summit would be especially difficult. It looked so from the distance, but when we came to it quite an easy way appeared of getting up. We stepped over one sharp knife-edged ridge, 'tight-rope dancing' we called it, and with a loud hurrah, reached the summit.... Would that many could see and experience the joy of this beautiful mountain as I have done. *Aufwiedersehen!*"

XI

AFIELD IN JASPER

Hitherto we have been wandering about what may be called the Southern Group of the Canadian National Parks, along the main line of the Canadian Pacific Railway. There remain two parks, Jasper and Robson, lying on either side of Yellowhead Pass, famous in the annals of the fur-trade as Tête Jaune. Through both run the lines of the new transcontinental railways, the Grand Trunk Pacific and the Canadian Northern, on their way to the Pacific coast. These two parks may for convenience be called the Northern Group, although only one is strictly speaking a national park, Robson being under the jurisdiction of the Provincial Government of British Columbia. Tête Jaune Pass and Tête Jaune Cache are said to commemorate the personality of a veteran Indian trader or trapper whose yellow hair made him conspicuous in a country where black was the prevailing hue. Jasper Park is named after a famous trader of the North West Company, Jasper Hawes, the site of whose trading fort may still be seen on the banks of the Athabaska, though every vestige of the buildings has long since disappeared. Jasper House, as it was called, was still standing when Milton and Cheadle went through the mountains in 1862. They describe it as "a neat white building, surrounded by a low palisade, standing in a perfect garden of wild flowers, backed by dark green pines which clustered thickly round the bases of the hills." Ten years later, when Sandford Fleming examined the pass as a possible route for the Canadian Pacific Railway, the post had been abandoned and the buildings were falling into decay. A mile or two east of Jasper, the headquarters of the park, one is shown a grassy mound which represents all that remains of another old trading post, Henry House. Here two routes through the mountains forked, one leading up to Yellowhead Pass, and the other to Athabaska Pass.

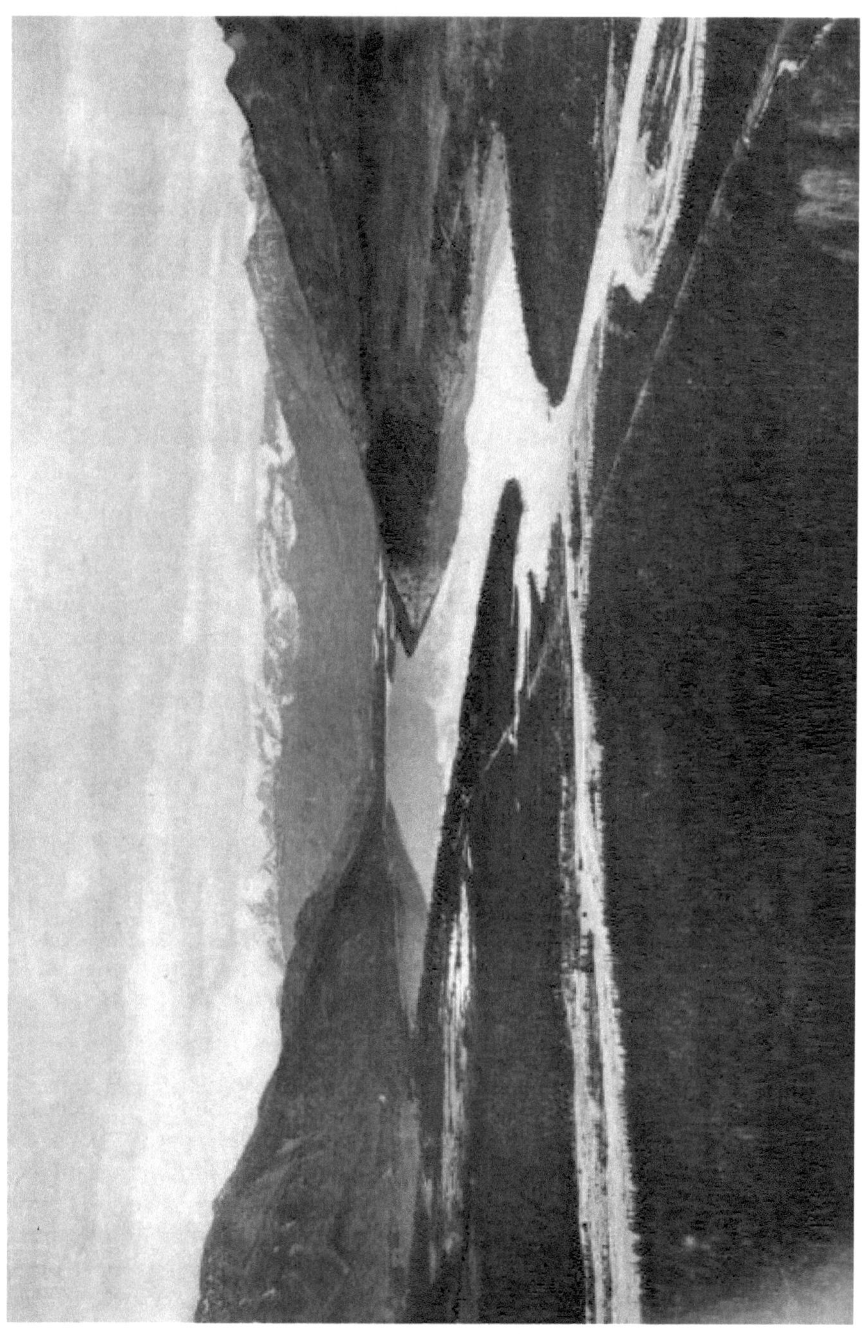

R. C. W. Lett

JASPER LAKE

The peculiar charm of Jasper Park, and of its sister reservation on the western side of the Pass, is in the fact that it is almost virgin ground. As a Park it is very young indeed, and there has not yet been time to improve upon nature. Lest this should suggest a touch of sarcasm, let us admit at once that nature can be improved upon when the improvement takes the form of practicable trails into the heart of the mountains, and the opening of such trails is one of the principal objects of the Canadian Parks authorities. Nevertheless, however one may appreciate the convenience of a good trail, there is a joy unspeakable to the natural man in getting out into the wilderness, if possible where no man has been before, but at least where nothing exists to remind him of the noisy civilisation he has managed to escape from for a time. And that is what you will find in Jasper Park: no automobiles, no stage coaches, no luxurious hotels, no newspapers, no luxuries of any kind, and very few conveniences; but a sufficiency of plain food, the intoxicating air of the mountains to eat it in, and the mountains themselves ever about and above you. What more could a tired man ask? What more could any man ask?

At least so two eastern city men thought as they awoke one glorious August morning to find their train crossing the eastern boundary of Jasper Park, with Brulé Lake sparkling ahead and the curious outlines of Folding Mountain dominating the landscape to the south. At a little station called Pocahontas, a few miles beyond the western end of the lake, they were dumped off unceremoniously with their luggage, and welcomed by a stalwart park officer who had rashly undertaken to look after them for the next few days, and particularly to pilot them out to the Miette hot springs. While he trotted off to round up his ponies, the two "tenderfeet" had leisure to look about them.

Pocahontas, what there is of it, nestles at the foot of Roche Miette, a great frowning bastion of rock dropping sheer for nearly a thousand feet toward the waters of the Athabaska. They tell you in the mountains that it was named after a trapper who managed to clamber up its precipitous sides many years ago, perhaps in chase of a mountain goat, and sat himself down on the extreme edge with his feet dangling over the thousand foot drop. No doubt the situation afforded him the same satisfaction that is experienced by those praiseworthy citizens whose names one sees carved on the extreme end of a log overhanging the Horseshoe Falls at Niagara. Posterity has rather a rude name for such heroes.

A short walk from Pocahontas brings you to a view of one of the most charming waterfalls in this part of the mountains. The erosion of ages has here carved out of the face of the cliff a lofty, semi-circular alcove, and over this background of sombre rock drops a ribbon of sparkling diamonds. An illustration might give some idea of the scene, but could not do justice to the peculiar grace and animation of the fall as seen under a bright sun and swayed gently by a summer's breeze. There are a number of beautiful waterfalls in Jasper Park, such as those on Stony River, a tributary of the Athabaska some distance above Pocahontas, in the Maligne Canyon, of which something will be said later, on the south side of Pyramid Mountain, and on Sulphur Creek above the hot springs, but none that cling to the memory like that of the Punch Bowl.

Largely because the Southern Parks, Rocky Mountains, Yoho and Glacier, are comparatively well known, the writer has preferred to describe them impersonally, to picture them as far as possible as seen through the eyes of other and more competent authorities, men who have learnt to know them intimately. The case is different with the Northern Parks, Jasper and Robson. Very few visitors from the outside world have yet discovered their wonderful possibilities; indeed until very lately they have been inaccessible except to those possessing the time and hardihood for a long journey from Edmonton over very rough trails. Similarly very little has been written about the Northern Parks. For this reason the writer will venture to describe in a more personal vein some of the characteristic features of Jasper and Robson.

Presently the ponies arrived, and we set off on our fourteen-mile ride to the Miette springs. The trail was a good one, so that we were not yet in the full enjoyment of the wilderness. That was to come later. Mile after mile we jogged along, sometimes in the open, sometimes in the heart of the woods, winding zigzag fashion down a steep hillside, splashing through a noisy little creek, and zigzagging up the opposite hill. For a couple of hours Roche Miette towered above us as we swung around his flank, and then ahead loomed up the great wall of Buttress Mountain, with Fiddle Creek winding along its base, peacefully enough now, so peacefully indeed that it is hard to believe the tales we are told of its resistless fury as it rages down in the spring, filling this wide channel from bank to bank, and turning its wonderful canyon—200 feet of sheer black rock—into a roaring hell of waters.

The Springs themselves we did not find particularly interesting. We listened respectfully to the information that their temperature ranged from 112 to 128 degrees Fahrenheit, and that they possessed valuable curative properties. After testing the upper pool we were willing to believe that the temperature was even worse than that, and not being rheumatic we accepted the curative properties without question but without enthusiasm. Still it was a pleasant enough place to loaf for a day or two, scrambling about the hills and exploring the upper waters of Sulphur Creek, and the lower pool turned out to be rather an agreeable thing to roll about in for a time before turning in to our tent for the night. The big mountains, however, were still ahead of us, and we saw the last of the little group of springs without much regret. Within a year or two the primitive pools that have cured the rheumatism and other ailments of generations of traders and trappers for a hundred years or more, will be confined in neat concrete basins, and a pipe line will carry the water down the valley of Fiddle Creek to the Château Miette, one of a series of great hotels that the Grand Trunk Pacific Railway is to build through the mountains. Never mind, the tourists are welcome to the Miette Hot Springs, and they may build an automobile road along the face of Buttress Mountain if they will, so that they leave us for a time unspoiled some of the wild spots that lie beyond.

We started back to Pocahontas rather late in the afternoon, and the sun went down as we climbed the last hill from Fiddle Creek. Over the shoulder of Buttress Mountain a graceful spire soared into the sky, and as we turned in our saddles to take a last look at it before following the trail into the woods, it grew so strangely and wonderfully luminous that we unconsciously pulled in our horses and stood there in silent amazement. Momentarily the light deepened, and golden shafts shot out into the velvet sky. Then as we gazed spell-bound, from the very heart of the golden crown, and immediately behind the glowing peak, there rose the silver moon, and hovered for an instant on the very summit of the mountain, a vision so glorious that it almost brought tears to one's eyes.

R. C. W. Lett

FIDDLE CREEK CANYON

An hour's ride by rail from Pocahontas carried us to Jasper, the headquarters of the park administration, a rudimentary town seated in a charming valley and surrounded by mountains, with the Athabaska sweeping by on its way down to the plains. From here we made several short trips, to Pyramid Lake and Pyramid Mountain, the former a characteristically beautiful tarn, and the latter a graceful peak with a variety of colouring rarely found in these mountains, reds and browns, blacks and greys, softly blended with the utmost perfection. On the way we had glimpses of a couple of lovely little lakes on the other side of the Athabaska, lying close together, one a bright blue and the other a most brilliant emerald. Behind them rose Maligne Mountain, with the valley of the Athabaska opening up to the southwest, a group of great peaks in the distance, and around to the west the majestic, snow-crowned peak, Mount Geikie.

Another day was spent in a long walk to the Maligne Canyon. We started under heavy clouds, which presently broke in rain, that slow, persistent sort of rain that never seems to tire. On we plodded for hours, determined to stick it out because we had been warned that we would certainly be driven back. And in the end we were rewarded with the Canyon, seen under most uncomfortable and depressing conditions, but compelling admiration for its gloomy splendour, its ebony walls so close together in spots that one could almost jump across, not merely perpendicular but sometimes overhanging, so that creeping to the edge and leaning over one looked down to the centre of the stream roaring a hundred feet or more below.

One other afternoon was devoted to a visit to Swift, the first and only settler in the pass. Swift came here many years ago, after an adventurous career in mining camps from Colorado to northern British Columbia. On a hunting or trading expedition through the mountains he discovered a beautiful little prairie, a few miles below where Jasper now stands, and then and there determined to make it his home. He came back, built a rude log shack, took unto himself a wife, and despite innumerable discouragements has managed to live happily and contentedly. Today he owns a good farm in the heart of the Rocky Mountains, with cattle and horses, and as both the great transcontinental railways have had to build through his property, Swift bids fair to end his days in wealth and prosperity. If wealth can make him any happier, he thoroughly deserves it for his pluck and perseverance under conditions that would have driven most men to despair. An afternoon spent at Swift's ranch, roaming with him about his own particular little canyon, or listening to his yarns of mountain and plain, mining camp, trapping, and hunting, told with all the spirit of a born story-teller, is an experience well worth remembering.

XII

OUT OF THE WORLD

CHATTING one evening with the genial Superintendent of Jasper Park, into whose sympathetic ear we had been pouring our ardent desire to see some portion of the mountains that was at least comparatively unknown, he replied: "I know the very place you want—Maligne Lake, off to the south of here. I can get you a good guide and outfit to-night, and you can start in the morning." The name did not sound very inviting; rather suggested that some one had seen the lake and condemned it. It appeared, however, that the name was really given to the river by which the waters of the lake are carried down to the Athabaska, and that the Indians had their own good reasons for pronouncing it "bad." We lived to commend their verdict. As for the lake, it would be as reasonable to call it "Maligne" as to give such a name to a choice corner of paradise. That, however, is getting a little ahead of the story.

The following morning the guide and his helper with the outfit were waiting for us on the other side of the Athabaska. We and our packs were punted across, the pack-horses were loaded, we climbed on our ponies and started off for the undiscovered country, as it pleased us to call it, with mountains smiling down upon us, a radiant sky overhead, and unutterable joy in our hearts.

The trail—it is painful to admit that there was a trail, and an excellent one at that—led up the valley of the Athabaska to Buffalo Prairie, where we made our first camp after an easy day's journey. Buffalo Prairie is a beautiful meadow set among the rolling hills that break the level of the long valley, with that first consideration to those who travel in the mountains, an abundance of feed for the horses, and with wonderful views of the great guardian peaks, Geikie, Hardisty, the Three Sisters, and a great company of glittering giants as yet unnamed. To one who comes from the east where every little hillock has its name, it is startling to find oneself gazing reverently at a majestic pyramid of rock and ice soaring a mile or so into the sky, and learn from the indifferent guide that it is merely one of the thousand nameless mountains.

The following morning we were off early, to the infinite disgust of the horses who were revelling in the good feed of the prairie. There was a long day's journey ahead up to and over Bighorn Pass, and a good deal of uncertainty as to where we might find any sort of a camping ground on the other side of the mountains. For a time we continued our way up the valley of the Athabaska, and then began the long slow climb up to the pass, over 8000 feet above the sea. As we topped one hill after another, sometimes travelling through patches of jack pine, sometimes up the dry bed of a mountain stream, there opened up new and ever more glorious views of the great ranges on either side. High up on the trail we had to turn aside to make room for a long pack train on its way down to Jasper. Hideous confusion would result if the two outfits were allowed to get entangled, only to be made right after much expenditure of time and pungent language. Finally the last pack-horse went by with a picturesque packer jogging along in the rear, and we began the last and heaviest grind up to the pass. The trail wound into the pass, and up and ever up, until we must get off the plucky little beasts and lead them the final stage, puffing and panting as we stumbled along through the heavy loose shale until at last we stood on the summit, and with a last glance back at the peaks off toward Athabaska Pass turned down through an alpine meadow, and in the midst of a swirling snowstorm, toward the valley of the Maligne.

For hours we toiled around the shoulders of hills of loose shale, or through miles of muskeg, or fallen timber, sometimes mounted, oftener on foot leading our hard-worked ponies, until at long last with the sun below the horizon we found on a steep hillside a little feed for the horses, and water for our kettles. The tent had to be pitched on the trail, the only relatively clear spot that could be found, and we trusted to Providence not to send another outfit along in the middle of the night to walk over us. It had been a long heavy day's travel, and after our supper of bannocks and bacon and a pipe we turned in and slept as only those may sleep who travel on the wilderness trail.

Our tent has been spoken of, but it was more properly a tepee—not the tepee that you see in pictures of Indian life, made of skins neatly sewn together and perhaps ornamented with rude drawings—but a modern compromise, of the old Indian form but made of strong cotton. Some of the guides in the mountains much prefer the tepee to the tent in any of its familiar forms. Others will have none of it. Our own experience led us to the conclusion that the tepee is without a rival in a good tepee country, that is one where suitable tepee poles are abundant, but there are occasions when you have to camp in a district where poles are as hard to find as needles in a haystack, and the resources of the language seem ludicrously inadequate as you limp about the camp in an ever-widening circle hunting for something that will support the thrice-damnable tepee for the night.

If you are fortunate enough to find a sufficient number of long, straight, slender poles among the fallen timber (in the parks you are not permitted to cut down trees for the purpose), it is a matter of but a very few minutes to stack them in position, stretch the cotton over the frame, and lace the front with a handful of small twigs, leaving an opening at the top. Then you make the beds around the circle, and build your camp fire in the middle. On a cold night, and particularly on a cold, rainy night, one blesses the Indian who first invented the tepee. Instead of shivering outside around a fire that will not burn, you have your fire with you in a large roomy tent, and can cook your meals and eat them in comfort. And who that has experienced it can forget the evening around the tepee fire, resting tired bodies on luxurious beds, smoking the pipe of peace, and swapping yarns until it is time to roll up in the thick, warm Hudson Bay blankets and sleep until dawn, or until the smell of frying bacon awakens one to another day's adventures.

H. W. Craver

MALIGNE LAKE

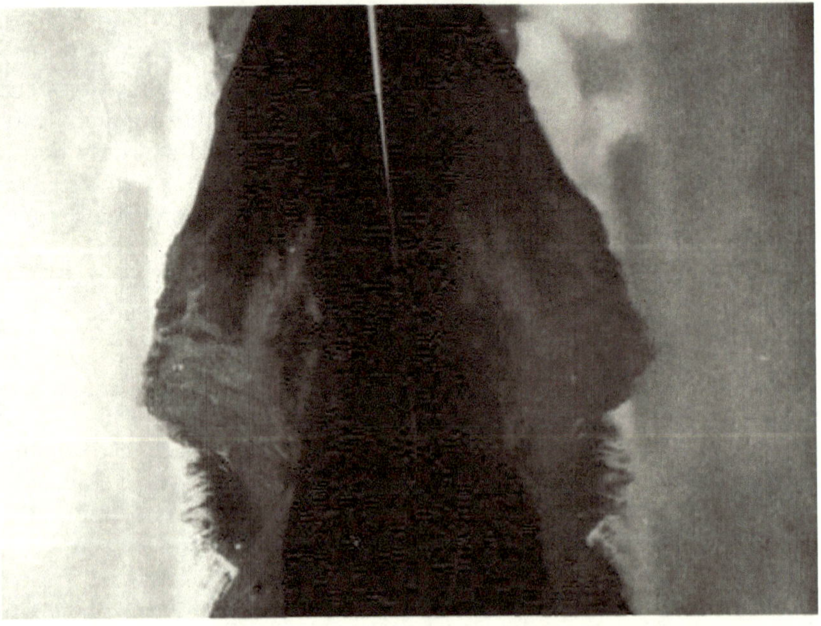

H. W. Craver

JACK LAKE

This morning on the hillside overlooking the Maligne Valley proved to be a Red Letter day in our calendar. The sun had been rather unkind since we left Jasper, but now as we scrambled out of the tepee, we looked up into a cloudless sky.

Far below a noisy little creek hailed us cheerily as it hurried down from the mountains to join the Maligne. In the distance we had glimpses of the river itself, and beyond uprose an extraordinary wall of rock a thousand feet or more in height, shutting in the valley and running on one side toward Maligne Lake and on the other far off into the hazy distance toward the Athabaska.

Our plans were to climb up the valley to Maligne Lake, take advantage of the kindly sun to secure a few pictures, and then make our way back to last night's camp and down the valley to Medicine Lake. East of Medicine Lake we had heard of a wonderful little body of water called Jack Lake, famous not so much because of its beauty as for the extraordinary abundance of its trout.

A ride of an hour or so, up and down hill, through fallen timber, muskeg and acres of boulders, with finally a most delightful gallop through a piece of virgin timber, brought us unexpectedly out on to a point of land overlooking Maligne Lake. We had read Mrs. Schäffer's enthusiastic description of the lake, but were hardly prepared for the perfectly glorious sight that lay before us: a lake of the most exquisite blue, mirroring on one side a high ridge clothed to the water's edge in dark green timber, and on the other a noble range of mountains climbing up and up in graceful towers and pinnacles sharply outlined against a cloudless sky. Beside us was an ideal camping ground, and then and there we vowed to come back to this spot some day, with several weeks to the good, and really make the acquaintance of Maligne Lake, if one must call anything so gracious and beautiful by such an inappropriate name.

Among the trees by the lake side we caught a glimpse of a tent, but the owner was nowhere in sight. We afterwards learned that he was one of the forest rangers, who rejoiced in the picturesque name of Arizona Pete. How Arizona Pete had wandered so far from the land of alkali plains and canyons no one seemed to know, but it was apparent that he had accumulated in his travels a fund of hair-raising stories of which Pete was the hero. If one heard of a riotously impossible exploit, and it was not attributed to that mythical hero of the northwest, Paul Bunion, one knew at once that it must be one of the adventures of Arizona Pete.

Turning our backs most reluctantly on Maligne Lake, we rode back to our deserted camp, and north toward Medicine Lake following what by courtesy was called a trail but was actually nothing but a few blazes pointing the way through a perfect wilderness of fallen timber. How the ponies, with all their marvellous intelligence and matchless endurance dragged themselves and us through the miles of hopelessly tangled logs that covered ridge and valley nearly every foot of the way to Medicine Lake, none of us could ever understand. However, we did at last reach the mouth of the river where it emptied into the lake.

Our proposed camping ground was in sight, a little cove on the eastern side of the lake, with feed of sorts for the horses, and the prospect of poles for the tepees; but we had still to cross the river and the situation looked discouraging. There was said to be a ford here, but the water had risen within the last few days and the sagacious ponies sniffed at it disapprovingly. We tried one place after another, until finally as a last resource the guide mounted the pluckiest and most sure-footed of the bunch and coaxed him out into the raging stream. Step by step they won their way to the other side, and the rest, having seen that the thing could be done, followed willingly enough. We all got over with nothing worse than a wetting, and the precious provisions escaped even that. Twenty minutes brought us to the camping ground, and our troubles were over for that day.

A plunge in the icy waters of Medicine Lake the following morning, followed by a hasty breakfast, and we were off for Jack Lake eight or ten miles to the east. The guide knew that the trail led off from a creek near the camp, but we must hunt for the exact spot where it began. It sounds simple enough, but in reality it was not at all simple. The trail had not been much used, and the creek from which it started ran through a dense thicket of alder. There was nothing to do but circle around until we found it. So we did, sometimes ploughing through the bush, sometimes splashing up the creek, until at last a cry from the guide told us that the elusive trail was found, and we could get on our way.

A few hundred yards brought us to the edge of the timber, and we plunged from bright sunlight into the shade of the primæval forest, where ancient cedars with venerable beards rose on every side from a carpet of deep, emerald moss. On we jogged for several miles, winding through the forest, now and then crossing a clear woodland stream, and climbing gradually up into a pass through the mountains. Presently we emerged from the trees with bold cliffs rising on either side carved into fantastic shapes. We dropped down into a secluded valley, with an emerald lake in the centre surrounded by velvet meadows, dark green timber beyond stretching up to the foot of white cliffs which rose abruptly on every side. Except for an eagle soaring far above there was no sign of life in the valley, and the silence was so absolute that one unconsciously lowered one's voice as if on the threshold of some awe-inspiring temple.

The trail led down the valley, skirting the shores of the lake, wandered through a bit of wood and brought us out on the shores of another lake, finally into the timber again, and up out of the valley through a gap in the mountains. Then for an hour or two we were lost in the forest, following the trail as it wound about and about in the seemingly casual and aimless fashion of wood trails. It did not appear at the moment very important that it should lead anywhere. The air was fragrant with the smell of pine and cedar and of a temperature that left absolutely nothing to be desired; the great trees were far enough apart to afford delightful vistas down long avenues whose mossy carpet was kissed by sunbeams filtering through the evergreen branches far above; the trail was clear and unencumbered, in wonderful contrast to our experience of the previous day; and we were quite content to jog along care-free and at peace with the world.

Finally a flash of blue through the trees warned us that we were drawing near Jack Lake. We followed its shore for a mile or so, or rather climbed along the face of the steep hillside that did duty for shore on this side, and rounding the eastern end came out on a broad meadow, with a new log shack in the foreground, a fringe of trees in the middle distance, and a noble range of mountains filling in the background. The owner of the shack, a young forest ranger, rushed out to welcome us with the almost pathetic exuberance of one who had not had anybody but his dog to talk to for several weeks.

A. Knechtel

BREAKING CAMP IN THE MOUNTAINS

A. Knechtel

MAKING A TRAIL THROUGH FALLEN TIMBER

When we had satisfied for the time his hunger for news of the outside world, we produced our rods and requested him to produce his trout. He grinned at the rods, and showed us his own—a stout stick with a heavy cord tied to one end, and at the end of the cord a bent horseshoe nail. "The bull trout here," he said, "don't like fancy rods." One of us stuck manfully to his treasured equipment; the other borrowed the ranger's stick and attached to it his heaviest line. Our hooks we learned were much too delicate for the purpose, but finally we managed to dig up a heavy pike hook for one line and a spoon for the other. With a lump of fat pork for bait, we followed the ranger down the banks of a creek running out of the lake, until we reached a deep, still pool. He pointed silently to the pool, and we gasped. The pool was literally alive with big trout from two to four or five pounds. The lines barely touched the water before there was a fierce rush. The trout were fighting for the bait. A huge fellow on each line, a brief struggle, and both were safely landed. Within ten minutes we had more than the party could eat in the next two or three days, and were throwing back all but the largest fish. The climax came when we ran out of pork, and one of us half jokingly made a cast with the spoon and no bait, and landed a 4-pounder on each naked hook. After that we gave it up, and tried the lake, hoping for trout that would give us something a little more like sport; but there for some reason or other, probably because the water in shore was shallow and we had no way of getting out into the lake, we ran to the other extreme, and had not a nibble in an hour's fishing. Although the story of our experience on the creek is absolutely authentic, we feel sadly enough that it is useless to hope that any one who has not visited Jack Lake will credit the story. The world is full of Doubting Thomases, and fish stories are fish stories. Nevertheless, this one is true.

The following morning we retraced our steps to Medicine Lake, and after several hours' most painful scrambling along its precipitous banks—where some enemy had told us there was a trail—we reached its northern end, and camped for the night. Maligne Lake and Medicine Lake drain into the Athabaska by Maligne River, but at the northern end of the second lake, where one would expect to find a considerable stream flowing out, the shore runs around smoothly to the western side without a break. The lake empties through a subterranean channel, and reappears in springs some miles down the valley, where the Maligne, hitherto a small creek, suddenly develops into a respectable river.

We had been advised to return to the Athabaska by a direct trail from Jack Lake, but our evil genius prompted us to try the Maligne River route which would bring us out near Jasper. Never did the shortest way round prove more conclusively the longest way home. For nine long hours we toiled down that interminable valley without rest or food, crossing the river back and forth innumerable times, scrambling up banks so steep that we had to go on hands and knees with our faithful little nags struggling up after us, and then finding in disgust that we had to slide down again to the rocky bed of the river, worrying through miles of fallen timber, miles of muskeg, miles of wiry bushes that slapped us viciously in the face as we forced a way through, and ripped our clothing until we looked more like stage tramps than fairly respectable travellers. The expected trail proved to be nothing but a few experimental blazes on the trees; experimental surely, as we found more than once to our cost, following the blazes to a standstill in a blind lead, and turning back in our tracks for perhaps half a mile to where the "trail" branched off to the other side of the valley. That day we became temporary converts to the theory that the pathless wilderness was no place for sane mortals.

However, every lane must have its turning, and at last we hailed with shouts of joy the familiar gorge of the Maligne, which we had visited from Jasper some time before. From the gorge over to the Athabaska we had a good trail, a boat ferried us across after our swimming horses, and we were back again at the Hotel Fitzhugh, raiding the neighbouring store for tobacco, our last pipeful having been smoked two days before. Probably this had more than a little to do with our gloomy impressions of the Maligne River trail.

XIII

THE MONARCH OF THE ROCKIES

WAVING a glad farewell to Jasper, the ugly little outpost of civilisation, we threw our bags on the west-bound train the following morning and were off for Mount Robson. A few miles' easy grade and we were at the summit of Yellowhead Pass, the continental divide. Behind us was Alberta, ahead British Columbia. We had left Jasper Park, and were entering Robson Park.

Sliding down the long slope of the Fraser valley, with the blue waters of Yellowhead Lake on our left hand, Mount Fitzwilliam above us to the south, and the loftier peak of Geikie gradually opening up beyond, we began to realise that there was much yet to be seen both at our feet and up in the clouds. Another ten or fifteen miles, and we were travelling along the north shore of Moose Lake, with the Rainbow Mountains on one side and the Selwyn Range on the other. Moose Lake was left behind, and we crowded out on to the rear platform of the train to get our first glimpse of the Monarch of the Rockies, Mount Robson. Almost without warning it came. We rounded the western end of the Rainbow Mountains and looked up the valley of the Grand Fork. "My God!" some one whispered. Rising at the head of the valley and towering far above all the surrounding peaks we saw a vast cone, so perfectly proportioned that one's first impression was rather one of wonderful symmetry and beauty than of actual height. Then we began to realise the stupendous majesty of the mountain, and recalled the words of Milton and Cheadle half a century ago, "a giant among giants, immeasurably supreme." Now, as then, its upper portion was "dimmed by a necklace of light feathery clouds, beyond which its pointed apex of ice, glittering in the morning sun, shot up far into the blue heaven."

It is interesting to know that David Douglas was not the only scientist who made a wild guess at the height of a Rocky Mountain peak. Douglas absurdly over-estimated the elevation of Mount Brown and Mount Hooker. Alfred R. C. Selwyn quite as absurdly under-estimated the height of Mount Robson, and he was at the time Director of the Geological Survey of Canada. Selwyn made an expedition to the upper waters of the Fraser in 1871, and in his official report says of Robson: "It rises with mural precipices to a height of two or three thousand feet above the river." As a matter of fact the summit of the peak is about ten thousand feet above the river, and something over thirteen thousand feet above the sea. There is comfort for the rest of us in the fact that such an eminent scientist as the late Dr. Selwyn could make such an extraordinary mistake.

Grand Trunk Pacific Railway Company

THE PURPLE CRAGS OF ROCHE MIETTE

(From a painting by George Horne Russell)

We escaped from the train at a little station named after the great mountain, and after several miles' tramp reached the base camp of the Alpine Club of Canada, which was then holding its annual meeting in the Robson district. There we spent the night, and before the sun went down were fortunate enough to get an unobstructed view of the peak, the last wisp of cloud driving off to the east leaving the mountain outlined from base to summit and glowing with unearthly radiance in the light of the setting sun. It is only at long intervals that such a view is to be obtained, the peak retiring for weeks at a time behind its curtain of clouds, or perhaps revealing its vast base and extreme summit while the upper slopes are hidden.

When we set out in the morning for the main camp of the Alpine Club by the shores of Berg Lake, on the north side of the mountain, Robson had vanished completely, so completely that a stranger coming here for the first time would not know that the impenetrable wall of cloud at the head of the valley hid anything more remarkable than the rugged hills on either side.

Our way lay for a time over the level ground covered with small timber; then the trail began to climb up the valley, and the next eight or ten miles developed into an almost continuous ascent, sometimes on easy grades, sometimes winding up the sides of a hill as steep as a high-pitched roof. At last beautiful Lake Kinney came in sight, with Robson rising in stupendous slopes and precipices and buttresses from its shores. Our way lay around the north shore of the lake, over a pebbly flat, around the shoulder of the mountain and into the Valley of a Thousand Falls—an enchanted valley, and we who had invaded it were nothing but dream-folk, wandering spell-bound among scenes more gorgeous than those of Sinbad the Sailor. Here was colour in riotous profusion, and form, of flower and tree, of sombre cliff and glittering snow-field and remote summit, music of mountain stream and waterfall, of waterfalls innumerable, and with it all a sublime spirit of rest and peace. What did it matter in this Vale of Content that beyond the outer mountains men were sweating and struggling for Dead Sea fruit. Here at least one could forget for the moment that he was one of the same folly-driven race.

Out of the valley at last we climbed, up and up past the Falls of the Pool and the Emperor Falls, up to the shores of Berg Lake whose sapphire waters are dotted with white craft launched from the eternal snows of the King of Mountains. Here at the end of a long day's journey, a journey overflowing with experience, we sat down to rest among the tents of the Alpine Climbers. Here, also, we listened to the story—surely one of fine pluck and endurance—of how George Kinney and Donald (popularly known as "Curlie") Phillips against all possible odds fought their way to the supreme peak of Robson. Let us hear it in their own words (*Alpine Club Journal*, 1910), only premising that this first ascent of the highest peak in the Canadian Rockies was made in August, 1909, after two unsuccessful attempts in 1907 and 1908, and that the final ascent was only accomplished after twenty days of continuous struggle, during which they were repeatedly driven back from the peak by impossible conditions.

R. C. W. Lett

MOUNT ROBSON

(*From the Grand Fork*)

"At last," says Mr. Kinney, "the weather began to clear up, and Monday, August 9th, we again climbed the rugged north shoulder. Crossing the difficult shale slope, we passed the camp spots of our former trips, and with our heavy fifty-pound packs struggled up those fearful cliffs till we reached an altitude of nearly ten thousand five hundred feet." Here they ran into a blizzard, and after a short, hopeless struggle, had to clamber down again to their base camp. Their provisions were almost exhausted, and they were many long miles from any possible source of supply. For three days it stormed, and they lived on birds and marmot. Finally on the 12th it cleared, and they again climbed to the top of the west shoulder. "Here, at an altitude equal to that of Mount Stephen, we chopped away a couple of feet of snow and ice, and feathered our nest with dry slate stones. We shivered over the little fire that warmed our stew, and then, amid earth's grandest scenes, we went to bed with the sun and shivered through a wretched night.

"Friday, August 13th, dawned cold and clear, but with the clouds gathering in the south. Using our blankets for a wind-brake we made a fire with a handful of sticks, and nearly froze as we ate out of the pot of boiling stew on the little fire. Then we laid rocks on our blankets so they would not blow away, and facing the icy wind from the south, started up the west side of the upper part of the peak. The snow was in the finest climbing condition, and the rock-work though steep offered good going. Rapidly working our way to the south, and crossing several ridges, we had reached in an hour the first of two long cliffs that formed horizontal ramparts all around the peak. We lost half an hour getting up this cliff.

"The clouds that came up with a strong south wind had gradually obscured the peak, till by the time we reached the cliff they were swirling by us on our level, and at the top of the cliff it began to snow. For a moment I stood silent, and then turning to my companion said: 'Curlie! my heart is broken.' For a storm on the peak meant avalanches on that fearful slope, and there would be no escaping them, so I thought that we would have to turn back, and our provisions were now so low that we would not have enough to make another two-day trip up the mountain. It meant that this was our last chance; but, to my surprise, it did not snow much, the clouds being mostly a dense mist. In a few minutes I said, 'Let us make a rush for the little peak,' meaning the north edge of the peak which was directly above us. 'All right,' said Curlie, from whom I never heard a word of discouragement, and away we started, keeping to the hard snow slopes. Though these were extremely steep, the snow was in such splendid condition that we could just stick our toes in and climb right up hand over hand.

"By the time we had conquered the second of the long ramparts of cliffs that form black threads across the white of the peak, we concluded that it was not going to snow very hard, as the clouds were mostly mist and sleet. Swinging again towards the south, we headed directly for the highest point of the mountain, which we could see now and then through the clouds. Small transverse cliffs of rock were constantly encountered, but they were so broken that we could easily get up them by keeping to the snow of the little draws.

R. C. W. Lett

EMPEROR FALLS

"For hours we steadily climbed those dreadful slopes. So fearfully steep were they that we climbed for hundreds of feet where standing erect in our footholds the surface of the slopes was not more than a foot and a half from our faces, while the average angle must have been over sixty degrees. There were no places where we could rest. Every few minutes we would make footholds in the snow large enough to enable us to stand on our heels as well as our toes, or we would distribute our weight on toe and hand-holds and rest by lying up against the wall of snow. On all the upper climb we did nearly the whole work on our toes and hands only. The clouds were a blessing in a way, for they shut out the view of the fearful depths below. A single slip any time during that day meant a slide to death. At times the storm was so thick that we could see but a few yards, and the sleet would cut our faces and nearly blind us. Our clothes and hair were one frozen mass of snow and ice.

"When within five hundred feet of the top, we encountered a number of cliffs covered with overhanging masses of snow, that were almost impossible to negotiate, and the snow at that altitude was so dry that it would crumble to powder and offer poor footing. We got in several difficult places that were hard to overcome, and fought our way up the last cliffs only to find an almost insurmountable difficulty. The prevailing winds being from the west and south, the snow driven by the fierce gales had built out against the wind in fantastic masses of crystal, forming huge cornices all along the crest of the peak, that can easily be distinguished from the mouth of the Grand Fork some ten miles away. We finally floundered through these treacherous masses and stood, at last, on the very summit of Mount Robson.

"I was astonished to find myself looking into a gulf right before me. Telling Phillips to anchor himself well, for he was still below me, I struck the edge of the snow with the staff of my ice axe and it cut in to my very feet, and through that little gap that I had made in the cornice, I was looking down a sheer wall of precipice that reached to the glacier at the foot of Berg Lake, thousands of feet below. I was on a needle peak that rose so abruptly that even cornices cannot build out very far on it. Baring my head, I said, 'In the name of Almighty God, by whose strength I have climbed here, I capture this peak, Mount Robson, for my own country and for the Alpine Club of Canada.'"

The descent was not accomplished without difficulty and danger, especially as a warm wind was melting the lower slopes and frequent detours had to be made to avoid places where the ice or rock beneath the thin snow would allow of no footholds whatever. It took five hours to climb to the summit from the camp on the top of the west shoulder, and seven hours to return to the same spot. During those twelve hours it was impossible either to eat or rest. It was long after dark before they reached the base camp, the entire climb occupying twenty hours. "We were so tired we could hardly eat or rest and our feet were very sore from making toe-holds in the hard snow. But we had stood on the crown of Mount Robson, and the struggle had been a desperate one. Three times we had made two-day climbs, spending ninety-six hours in all above ten thousand feet altitude, so far north. During the twenty days we were at Camp Robson we captured five virgin peaks, including Mount Robson, and made twenty-three big climbs."

XIV

ON THE MOOSE RIVER TRAIL

A PLEASANT evening had been spent on the shores of Berg Lake, admiring the wonderful views of Robson and its encircling glaciers, with Mount Resplendant, the Dome and the Helmet, Whitehorn Peak off to the right, Rearguard immediately over Berg Lake, Ptarmigan Peak to our left, and Mount Mumm, named after the well-known English Alpine climber, behind us; surely an unrivalled collection of gigantic ice-crowned peaks, encircling one of the most beautiful lakes in the world. A few days before two members of the Alpine Club with the Swiss guide Konrad Kain had climbed to the summit of Robson, and while we were in camp another party came down, unsuccessful, after three days spent on the peak. They had been driven back when within a few hundred feet of the summit by a dangerous snow storm. After the sun went down we walked over to the big camp-fire of the Alpine Club, and listened to the climbing experiences of the mountaineers, regretting that our plans would not permit us to join one of the parties in an attack on one of the less formidable peaks.

Through the good offices of the Superintendent of Jasper Park, we had been fortunate enough to secure the services of Fred Stephens to take us through the Moose River country. So much has been said about guides, that it may not be amiss to explain, for the benefit of those who are not familiar with the Canadian Rockies, that there are two quite distinct classes of mountain guides, one possessing special knowledge of the high peaks and how to get up them, the other knowing like a book the intricate wilderness that lies about their feet. The climbing guides are Swiss, trained in the Alps. Two or three of them were engaged by the Canadian Pacific Railway some years ago, when mountain climbers first began to realise the splendid possibilities of the country about Laggan, Field and Glacier. The guides spent the summer in the Rockies, and returned to Switzerland for the winter. Since then the number has steadily increased, and now many of the Swiss guides have settled permanently in the Canadian Alps, which are now rapidly becoming popular as a winter as well as a summer resort.

R. C. W. Lett

MOUNT ROBSON FROM THE NORTHEAST

The trail guides are an entirely different class of men. They belong to the west, have been trained there, and know its ways. Some of them have been trappers or traders, many are hunters, and not a few have been cowboys, or miners. All know the mountains and the mountain trails, and most of them are good companions either in camp or on the trail, quietly competent when work is to be done, resourceful in the innumerable emergencies of mountain travel, and a fountain of shrewd wisdom and anecdote around the camp fire. And of all trail guides in the Canadian Rockies none is the superior of Fred Stephens, whether as guide, philosopher or comrade. We who had heard his praises sung by others, congratulated ourselves when we learned that he was to take us through the Moose River country.

Early next morning we were up and doing. Breakfast was despatched, the tents struck, the horses driven in to camp, packs made up and securely fastened to the backs of the pack-horses by means of the famous diamond hitch, our own ponies saddled, and we were off for Moose Pass, waving a reluctant farewell to our hosts of the Alpine Club as we trotted through the camp—a tent city gay with bunting, and instinct with the wholesome enthusiasm, good-fellowship, and hospitality of the mountaineers.

As we crossed the slight ridge at the foot of Robson Glacier, which at this point forms the continental divide, we paused to study for a moment the curious family history of two great water systems, born in the same glacier. From two blue ice caves in the Robson Glacier, one on either side of the ridge of the terminal moraine, flow two sparkling streams. One flows southwest into Berg Lake, the Grand Fork, the Fraser, and the Pacific Ocean; the other flows northeast into Lake Adolphus, the Smoky, Peace River, Slave River, Great Slave Lake, the Mackenzie, and the Arctic Ocean. Turning our backs on the Berg Lake tributary, after wishing it a pleasant journey to the Pacific, we followed its brother down to Lake Adolphus and for some miles beyond, when we turned east up Calumet Creek toward Moose Pass.

Near the summit of the pass we found ourselves in the midst of one of the most exquisite of Alpine meadows. Imagine a great bowl of dark rock relieved here and there with patches of fresh snow, and at the foot of this bowl a soft emerald carpet, the green almost hidden by glowing patches of flowers, asters and arbutus and harebell, purple and white heather, lady's tresses and columbine, moss campion, the twin flower and the forget-me-not. Think of it, you who treasure a little patch of forget-me-nots in your garden, think of walking your horse reverently through an acre of forget-me-nots, growing so thickly that the blue of them could be seen long before one reached the place where they grew, so thickly that one was compelled to the sacrilege of treading down thousands of blossoms as we crossed the meadow. In honour of the lady of our party, whom we believed to be the first white woman to pass this way, we named this beautiful spot Merwin Meadow.

Before we leave the meadow, listen for a moment to a writer who combines the imagination of a poet with the exact knowledge of a scientist, Dr. A. P. Coleman:

"If one halts by chance anywhere on a mountain pass, all sorts of thrilling things are going on around. Lovely flowers are opening eagerly to the sun and wind of Spring—in mid-August, with September's snows just at hand, a whole year's work of blossom and seed to be accomplished before the ten months' winter sleep begins. Bees are tumbling over them intoxicated with honey and the joy of life while it is summer. Even the humming-birds, with jewels on their breast as if straight from the tropics, are not afraid to skim up the mountain sides, poise over a bunch of white heather, and pass with a flash from flower to flower. The marmots with aldermanic vests are whistling and 'making hay while the sun shines,' and one may see their bundles of choice herbs spread on a flat stone to dry, while the little striped gophers are busy too. Time enough to rest in the winter.

R. C. W. Lett

MOOSE RIVER FALLS

"Everything full of bustle and haste and of joy, what could be more inspiring than the flowery meadows above tree-line when the warm sun shines in the six weeks of summer! The full splendour and ecstasy of a whole year's life piled into six weeks after snow has thawed and before it falls again!

"Higher up even the snow itself is alive with the red snow plant and the black glacier flea, like the rest of the world making the most of summer; and as you take your way across the snow to the mountain top, what a wonderful world opens out! How strangely the world has been built, bed after bed of limestone or slate or quartzite, pale grey or pale green or dark red or purple, built into cathedrals or castles, or crumpled like coloured cloths from the rag-bag, squeezed together into arches and troughs, into V's and S's and M's ten miles long and two miles high; or else sheets of rock twenty thousand feet thick have been sliced into blocks and tilted up to play leapfrog with one another.

"And then the sculpturing that is going on! One is right in the midst of the workshop bustle where mountains are being carved into pinnacles, magnificent cathedral doors that never open, towers that never had a keeper—all being shaped before one's eyes of the mighty beds and blocks of limestone and quartzite that were once the sea bottom. You can watch the tools at work, the chisel and gouge, the file and the sandpaper. All the workmen are hard at it this spring morning in August; the quarryman Frost has been busy over night, as you hear from the thunder of big blocks quarried from the cliffs across the valley; there is a dazzling gleam on the moist, polished rocks which Craftsman Glacier has just handed over to the daylight; and you can watch how recklessly the waterfall is cutting its way down, slicing the great banks of rock with canyons! It is inspiring to visit the mountains any day in the year, but especially so in the July or August springtime, when a fresh start is made, and plants, animals, patient glaciers, hustling torrents, roaring rivers, shining lakes are all hard at work rough-hewing or putting finishing touches on an ever new world."

We tried to keep our minds on such thoughts as these, as we left the meadow behind and crossed a ridge of most abominably sharp scree, hard on our feet and footwear as we trudged sulkily through it, and still harder on the unshod horses who followed patiently after. The ridge led to a long slope down the British Columbia side of the pass—for between the foot of Robson Glacier and Moose Pass we had crossed a wedge of Alberta—and then mile upon mile of muskeg, where as we floundered slowly ahead we alternately admired Fred Stephens' unerring skill in following a trail that only became faintly visible for a foot or two every three or four hundred yards, and damned him heartily for leading us into such a slough of despond. However, even the worst muskeg must have an end, and at last we and our weary horses pulled out on the other side, trotted happily through a bit of virgin forest, and cheered the guide when he pointed ahead to our camping ground, an ideal spot in a clearing beside the East Branch of the Moose River. We had made twenty miles from Berg Lake, pretty good going in such a country, a third of the journey being through heavy muskeg; and our second meal that day was at seven in the evening. Fred Stephens is without a peer as a guide, but he would never qualify as instructor in a cooking school. Nevertheless his bannocks that night seemed to us the very food of the gods. It may have been because he made them in a gold pan, or it may have been the dry humour of his stories, or perhaps it was the fact that breakfast seemed so remote that we had forgotten the existence of such a meal, but the fact remains that that luncheon-supper of bannocks and bacon left us at peace with the world.

Behind the camp rose an attractive little mountain offering some rather interesting rock climbing, and one of us made up his mind to have a try at it the following morning before breakfast. He managed to get into his clothes without disturbing the rest of the party, and pocketing a cold bannock started off for the mountain. The first obstacle appeared in the shape of a lively branch of the Moose, which had not been noticed the night before. A rapid survey up and down stream revealed no means of getting across dry, and there was nothing for it but to plunge in and wade across. It was waist deep in midstream, and the water was not only wet but most exceedingly cold. However, there was exercise enough ahead to overcome the chill of the reception.

A long scramble up a slope covered with closely matted bushes led at last to the rocks, and the rocks to a series of ledges. Being a novice, the climber lost much time in searching for practicable routes to the summit, and in an attempt to get up a chimney sent down such an avalanche of rock that the camp was aroused and began to contemplate a searching expedition for the remains of a fool climber. However, fate had some other end in view, and the climber went on his way. A steep slope of very fine, loose shale ending in a sheer drop of some hundred feet finally brought him to a standstill. He had little more than an hour to get back to camp, and it would take all of that to find another way up to the summit. That little mountain remained unconquered. He scrambled down to a draw between the hills, crossed a snow patch, swung down a long slope, plunged through the uninviting creek, and was back in time to find the party packed and ready to march.

Our way lay down the East Branch, partly over a fairly good trail, partly through a repetition of yesterday's muskeg. One of the pack-horses took it into his head to do pioneer work in opening up new trails through the bush, and was sent in disgrace to the rear of the string where the guide's helper could keep a watchful eye on him. The helper was a plucky but inexperienced little chap, and his limited vocabulary filled the pack-horses with contempt. Throughout that day we who were ahead with the guide could hear every little while far in the rear the faint cry, "Buckskin! Oh, Bu-u-ck-skin!" Finally the cry changed to, "O Fred! Pack's off!" and the philosophic guide cantered back to bring pack and pack-horse together again. Nothing could possibly look more meek and inoffensive than the mild-eyed Buckskin when he marched into camp that night, but he had given more trouble than the rest of the thirteen horses combined. He probably said to himself that he was a horse ahead of his generation, and that pioneers were generally misunderstood.

R. C. W. Lett

SWIMMING THE ATHABASKA

R. C. W. Lett

MAKING CAMP

We camped on the West Branch of the Moose, about a mile above its junction with the East Branch, having again made twenty miles from our last camp. Once more we camped by the river's side, with a fine range of mountains opposite, and a splendid view of the Reef Glaciers at the head of the valley. Resplendent and Robson were off to the west, but hidden behind intervening ridges. We had been hoping all day to see mountain goat, but found nothing but a wisp of wool on a bush above a salt lick.

The following morning we started down the Moose, with a succession of beautiful views up and down the valley. A deep creek which had been roughly bridged with logs gave us some trouble. One of the pack-horses—not the unfortunate Buckskin—went through, and it needed the united exertions of four men to get him out. The other horses, who had seen the accident and were still on the wrong side of the stream, refused to have anything to do with the bridge, and even after we had repaired it they were only with the utmost difficulty coaxed across one at a time.

Finally we topped the last ridge, and looked down into the valley of the Fraser. The railway track, looking like a thread in the distance, seemed utterly unfamiliar after our few days on the trail. We had made a wide circle around Robson, starting from Robson station, and coming back to the railway at what was known to the construction gangs as "Mile 17." We had supper in Reading's Camp, near the mouth of Grant Brook, and took the eastbound train back to Jasper.

A day or two later we turned our faces toward the east, leaving behind more than one friend that we had learned to know and appreciate in the simple, human life of trail and camp-fire; and carrying with us eternal memories of this region of glorious mountains and pine-scented valleys, lakes of turquoise and emerald, rushing crystal streams, waterfalls innumerable, glaciers and snow-fields, rugged cliffs and green-clad slopes, rock-strewn ridges and flower-bedecked meadows, and of the marvellously clear and intoxicating air of the mountains lifting the soul out of the mire and attuning it to a purer and more noble outlook. We had had glimpses of these wonderlands of the Canadian West, and we were resolved that another day should see our footsteps once more turned toward the beckoning hills.

To-day, with the "storm-winds of autumn" rushing by from the east, we feel like saying, with Matthew Arnold:

> "Ye are bound for the mountains—
> Ah, with you let me go
> Where your cold distant barrier,
> The vast range of snow,
> Through the loose clouds lift dimly
> Its white peaks in air—
> How deep is their stillness!
> Ah, would I were there!"

BIBLIOGRAPHY

BUTLER, WILLIAM FRANCIS. The Wild Northland. 1873.

BROWN, STEWARDSON, AND SCHAFFER, MRS. CHARLES. Alpine Flora of the Canadian Rocky Mountains. 1907.

COLEMAN, A. P. The Canadian Rockies. 1912.

COUES, ELLIOTT. New Light on the Early History of the Greater Northwest. The Manuscript Journals of Alexander Henry and David Thompson, 1799-1814. 1897.

COX, ROSS. Adventures on the Columbia River. 1831.

DAWSON, GEORGE M. The Canadian Rocky Mountains. 1886.

DAWSON, GEORGE M. Exploration from Fort Simpson to Edmonton. In Geological Survey of Canada Report, 1879-80.

DE SMET, PIERRE JEAN. Oregon Missions and Travels over the Rock Mountains in 1845-46. Reprinted as Vol. XXIX of Early Western Travels. 1906.

DOUGLAS, DAVID. Journey to Hudson's Bay. Companion to Botanical Magazine, II, pp. 135-38.

ERMATINGER, EDWARD. York Factory Express. In Transactions Royal Society of Canada, 1912.

FAY, CHARLES E. Rocky Mountains of Canada. Alpina Americana, No. 2 (1911).

FLEMING, SANDFORD. England and Canada. A Summer Tour between Old and New Westminster. 1884.

FOOTNER, HULBERT. New Rivers of the North. 1912.

FRANCHÈRE, GABRIEL. Narrative of a Voyage to the Northwest Coast of America in the years 1811-1814. 1854.

FRASER, SIMON. Journal of a Voyage from the Rocky Mountains to the Pacific Coast, 1808. In Masson, Bourgeois de la Compagnie du Nord-ouest. 1889.

GORDON, DANIEL M. Mountain and Prairie. 1830.

GRANT, GEORGE M. Ocean to Ocean. Sandford Fleming's Expedition through Canada in 1872. 1873.

GREEN, W. S. Among the Selkirk Glaciers. 1890.

GROHMAN-BAILLIE, W. A. Camps in the Rockies. 1883.

GROHMAN-BAILLIE, W. A. Fifteen Years' Sport and Life in Western America. 1900.

GROHMAN-BAILLIE, W. A. Seven Years' Path-finding in the Selkirks of Kootenay. In *Field*, May 11, 1899.

HARMON, DANIEL WILLIAMS. A Journal of Voyages and Travels in the Interior of North America. 1820.

HENSHAW, JULIA W. Mountain Wild Flowers of America. 1906.

HORETZKY, CHARLES. Canada on the Pacific. 1874.

HORNADAY, W. T., and PHILLIPS, JOHN M. Camp-fires in the Canadian Rockies. 1906.

HUBBARD, J. H. Sport in the Canadian Northwest. 1886.

KANE, PAUL. Wanderings of an Artist among the Indians of North America. 1859.

McARTHUR, J. J. Topographic Survey of the Rocky Mountains. In Reports Interior Department of Canada, 1887 and 1892.

McCONNELL, R. G. Geological Structure of a Portion of the Rocky Mountains. In Geological Survey of Canada Report, 1886.

McEVOY, JAMES. The Yellowhead Pass Route from Edmonton to Tête Jaune Cache. In Geological Survey of Canada Report, 1898.

MACKENZIE, ALEXANDER. Voyages from Montreal through the Continent of North America to the Frozen and Pacific Oceans, in 1789 and 1793. 1801.

McLEOD, MALCOLM. Peace River. A Canoe Voyage from Hudson's Bay to Pacific, by the late Sir George Simpson, in 1828. 1872.

MENNELL, H. T. Across Canada to the Rocky Mountains. 1885.

MILTON, VISCOUNT, and CHEADLE, W. B. The North-West Passage by Land. 1865.

MOBERLY, WALTER. The Rocks and Rivers of British Columbia. 1885.

OUTRAM, JAMES. In the Heart of the Canadian Rockies. 1905.

PALLISER, JOHN. Journals ... relative to Exploration ... between Lake Superior and the Pacific Ocean, 1857-60. 1863.

PALMER, HOWARD. Notes on the Exploration and the Geography of the Northern Selkirks. In Bulletin of the American Geographical Society, 1912.

PALMER, HOWARD. Mountaineering and Exploration in the Selkirks. 1914.

SCHAFFER, MARY T. S. Old Indian Trails. 1911.

SELWYN, ALFRED R. C. Explorations in British Columbia. In Geographical Survey of Canada Report, 1875-76.

SELWYN, ALFRED R. C. Preliminary Exploration in British Columbia. In Geographical Survey of Canada Report, 1871-72.

SHERZER, W. H. Glaciers of the Canadian Rockies or Selkirks. In Smithsonian Contributions to Knowledge, 1907.

SIMPSON, SIR GEORGE. Narrative of a Journey Round the World During the Years 1841 and 1842. 1847.

SOUTHESK, EARL OF. Saskatchewan and the Rocky Mountains. 1875.

STUTFIELD, H. E. M. and COLLIE, J. N. Climbs and Explorations in the Canadian Rockies. 1903.

WALCOTT, CHARLES D. The Monarch of the Canadian Rockies. In *National Geographic Magazine*, May, 1913.

WASHBURN, STANLEY. Trails, Trappers and Tender-feet in Western Canada. 1912.

WHEELER, A. O. and PARKER, ELIZABETH. The Selkirk Mountains, a Guide for Mountain Pilgrims and Climbers. 1911.

WHEELER, A. O. The Mountains of the Yellowhead Pass. In *Alpine Journal*, 1913.

WHEELER, A. O. The Selkirk Range. 1905.

WILCOX, W. D. Camping in the Canadian Rockies. 1896.

WILCOX, W. D. A Guide Book to the Lake Louise Region. 1909.

WILCOX, W. D. Picturesque Landscapes in the Canadian Rockies. 1898.

WILCOX, W. D. The Rockies of Canada. 1909.

Reference may also be made to the *Canadian Alpine Journal* and *Appalachia* containing many important articles on mountain-climbing in the Rockies and Selkirks, the geology, fauna and flora of the region, etc.; also to the Annual Reports of the Commissioner of Dominion Parks.

MAPS[4]

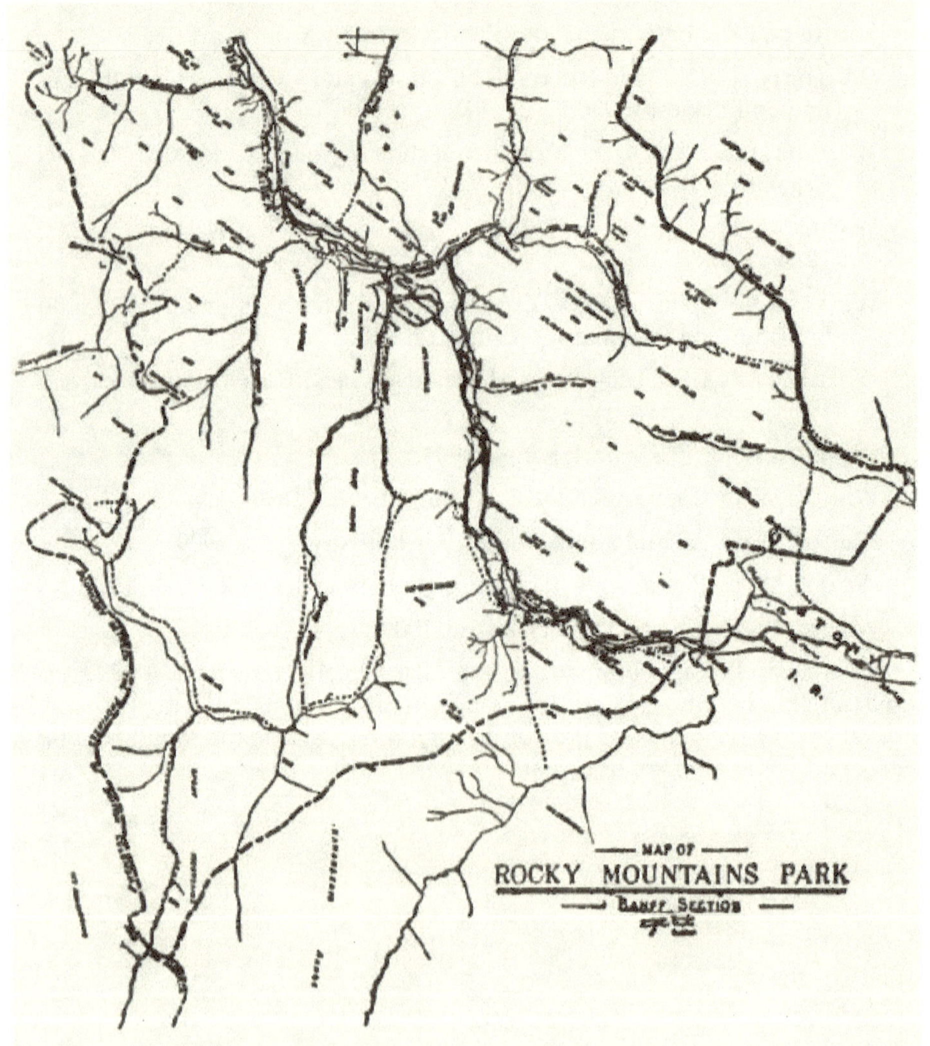

ROCKY MOUNTAINS PARK, BANFF SECTION

[4] Readers may note that the detailing of the maps could not be rendered as the original manuscript didn't include detailed layout of the maps.

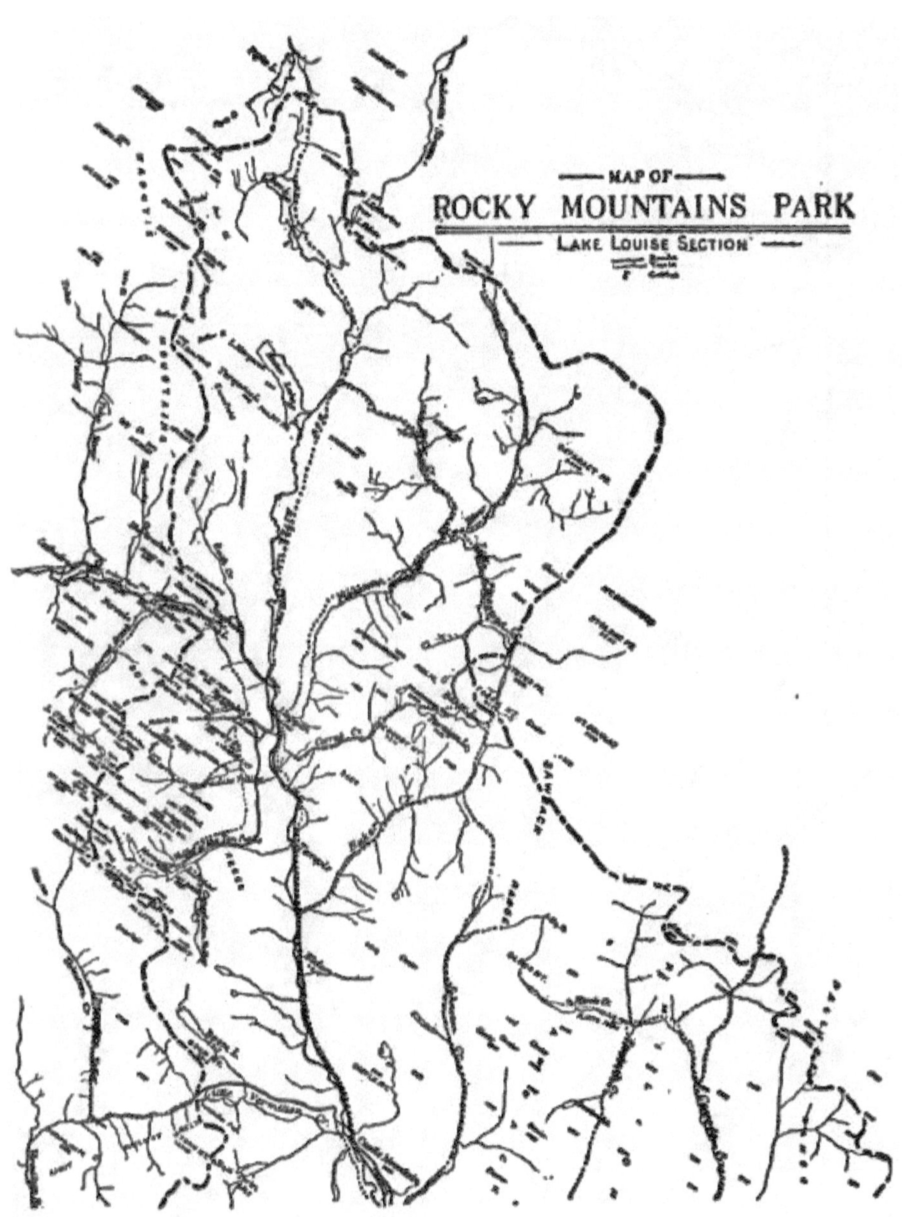

ROCKY MOUNTAINS PARK, LAKE LOUISE SECTION

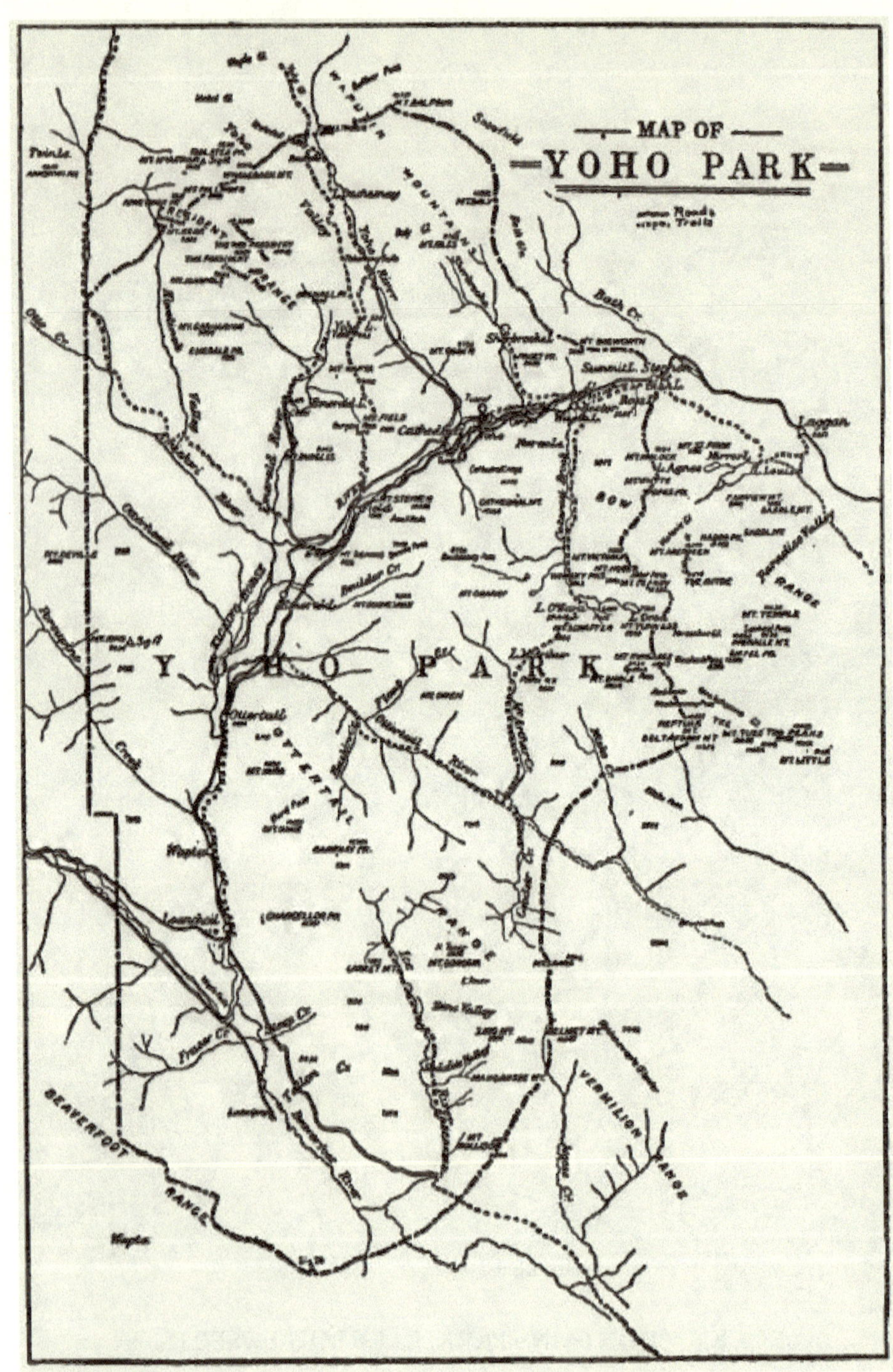

MAP OF
YOHO PARK
Roads
Trails
YOHO PARK
BEAVERFOOT RANGE
VERMILION RANGE
OTTERTAIL RANGE
VAN HORNE RANGE

YOHO PARK

JASPER PARK
ATHABASKA FOREST
ROCKY
MOUNTAINS
JASPER PARK
FOREST
RESERVE
BRAZEAU
FOREST
ROCKY

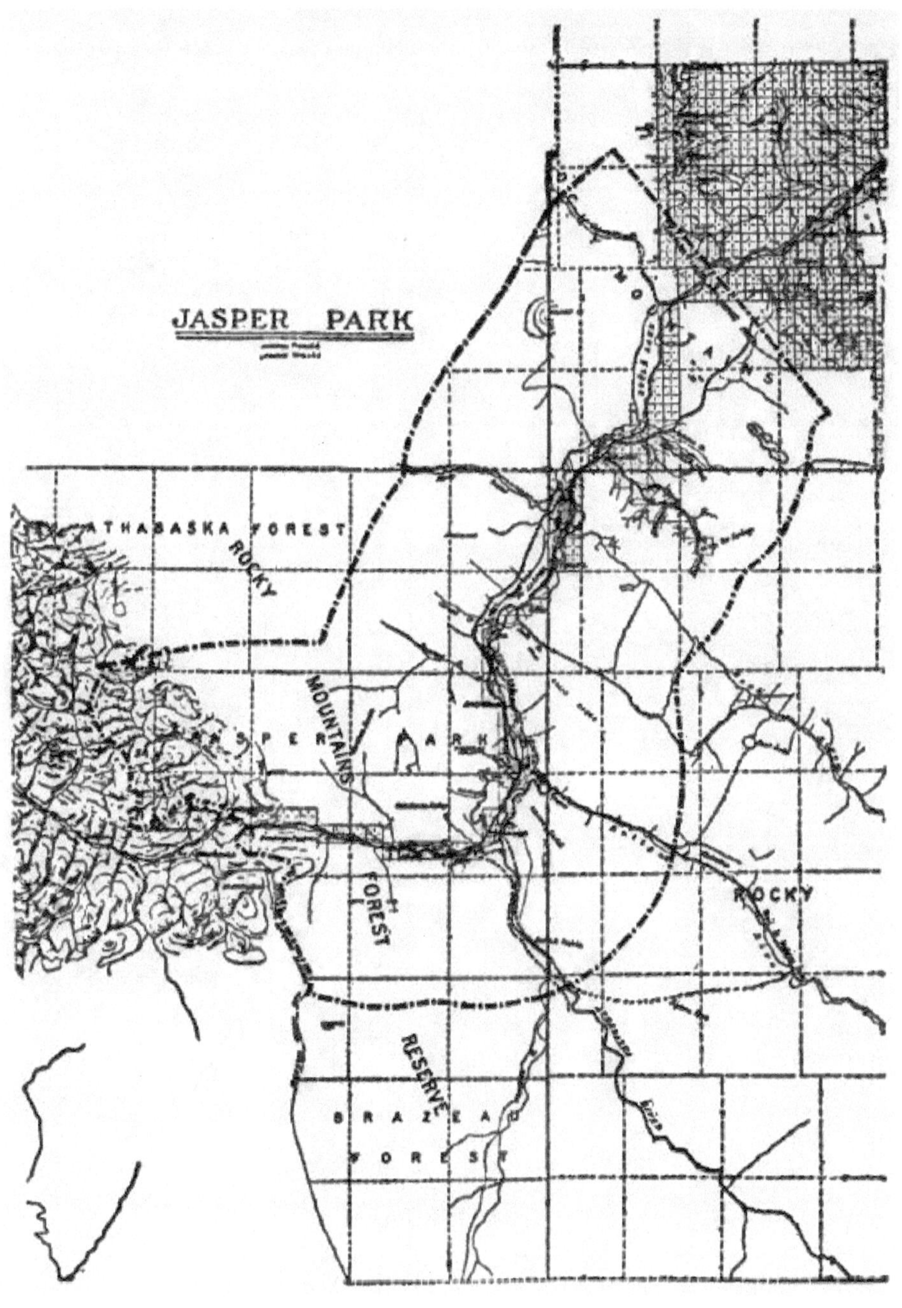

JASPER PARK

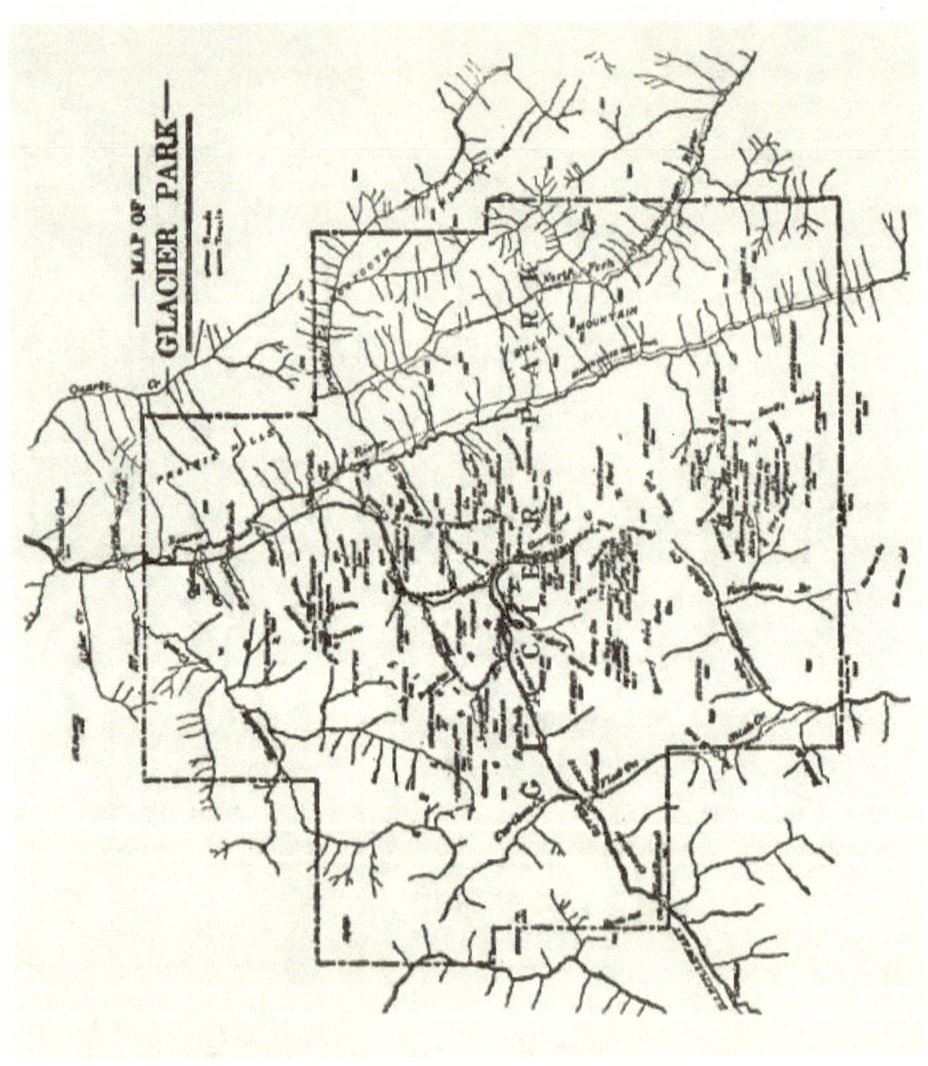

GLACIER PARK

ROCKY
MOUNTAINS
ATHABASKA FOREST
ROBSON PARK
British Columbia

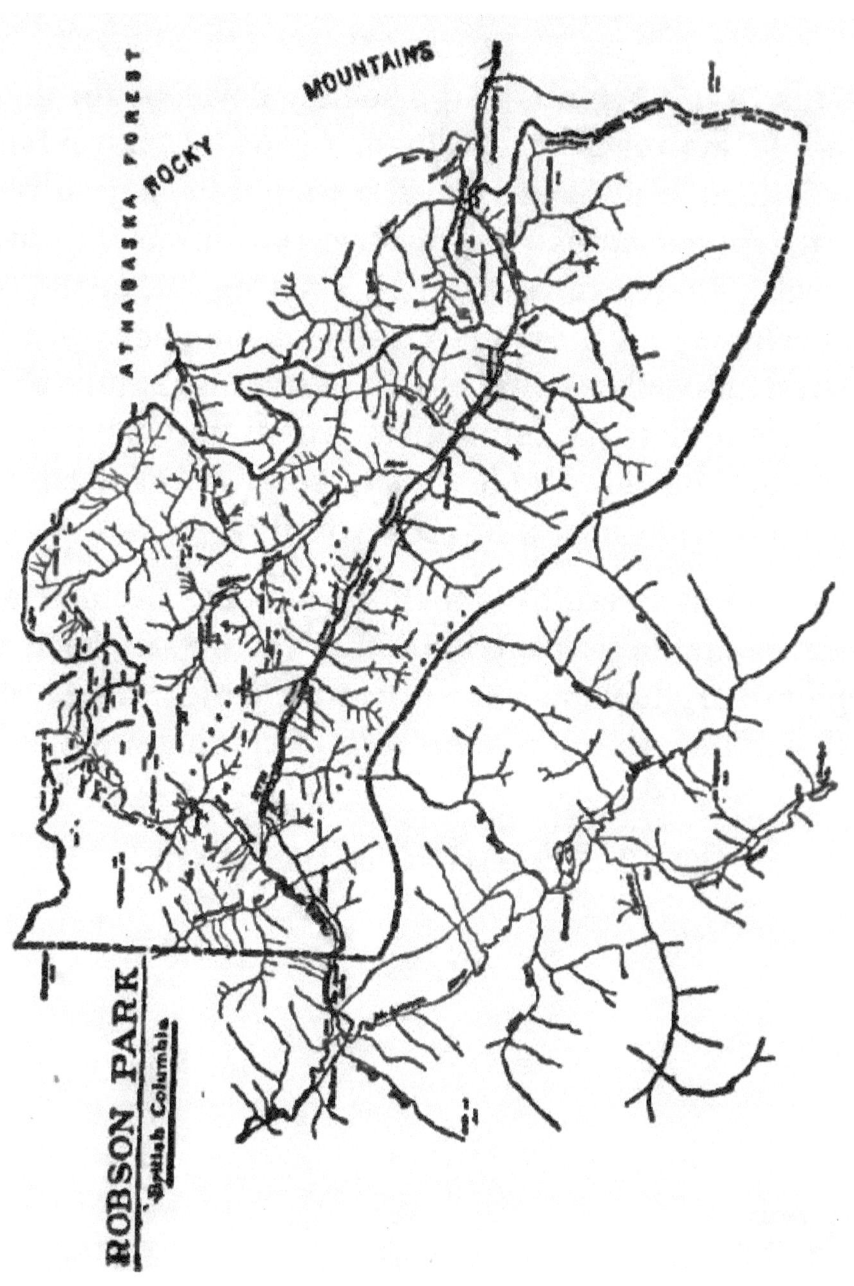

ROBSON PARK

Lector House believes that a society develops through a two-fold approach of continuous learning and adaptation, which is derived from the study of classic literary works spread across the historic timeline of literature records. Therefore, we aim at reviving, repairing and redeveloping all those inaccessible or damaged but historically as well as culturally important literature across subjects so that the future generations may have an opportunity to study and learn from past works to embark upon a journey of creating a better future.

This book is a result of an effort made by Lector House towards making a contribution to the preservation and repair of original ancient works which might hold historical significance to the approach of continuous learning across subjects.

HAPPY READING & LEARNING!

LECTOR HOUSE LLP
E-MAIL: lectorpublishing@gmail.com

www.ingramcontent.com/pod-product-compliance
Lightning Source LLC
LaVergne TN
LVHW090007200726
843493LV00004B/800